IMAGINATION AND FANCY

Imagination and Fancy

Complementary Modes in the
Poetry of Wordsworth

JAMES SCOGGINS

UNIVERSITY OF NEBRASKA PRESS · LINCOLN

Publishers on the Plains
UNP

Copyright © 1966 by the University of Nebraska Press
All rights reserved
Library of Congress Catalog Card Number 66–10879

Manufactured in the United States of America

For Ann

Acknowledgment

The Romantic period has been blessed with excellent scholars and critics, particularly in recent years, and these men and women are chiefly responsible for any value the present book might have. I have tried to acknowledge specific debts in the text and notes, but doubtless many insights of earlier writers on Wordsworth and his age have become so much a part of my thinking that I am no longer aware of their origin.

In one way or another many of my teachers, colleagues, and students have contributed to my understanding of Romantic poetry, but I can mention only a few here. I am happy to express my thanks for their invaluable advice and criticism to Bernice Slote, Samuel Holt Monk, Leon Gottfried, Donald H. Reiman, and Jack Stillinger; and to two of my students, Paul Magnuson and David Wiener. I also wish to thank the staffs of the Illinois, Minnesota, Cornell, and Houghton libraries for their considerable help and kindness, with special thanks to Eva Faye Benton and George H. Healey. Finally, it is a pleasure to record my greatest debts—to Royal A. Gettmann, for his unfailing wisdom and inspiration at every stage in the preparation of this book, and to my wife, for her patience, encouragement, and understanding.

   This study was furthered by generous grants from the English Department Research Committee of the University of Illinois and from the Graduate School and the McMillan Fund of the University of Minnesota.

J. S.

Contents

IMAGINATION AND FANCY

Introduction

One mark of great poetry is its ability to gain the admiration of readers who reject the premises on which it was constructed. Thus today William Wordsworth is respected by critics whose attitudes and beliefs he would have deplored, while the specific doctrines which he hoped to promote in his poems have practically disappeared from the thoughts of all but Wordsworthian scholars.

To disentangle art and dogma is of course an important function of criticism, but there is reason to wonder whether sometimes the separation may not be carried too far. A case in point is Wordsworth's painstaking effort to trace in his poems "the primary laws of our nature."[1] His most carefully contrived efforts in this direction are his descriptions of the two chief poetic faculties, imagination and fancy, and the classification of a number of his poems "with

---

[1] *The Poetical Works of William Wordsworth,* ed. Ernest de Selincourt and Helen Darbishire (rev. ed.; Oxford: Oxford University Press, 1952–1959), II, 386. Unless otherwise indicated all quotations from Wordsworth's poems and prefaces are taken from this edition, hereafter cited as *PW.* I have used this edition for convenience, but I have also consulted all editions supervised by Wordsworth himself. In the interest of clarity I have sometimes regularized the erratic punctuation of Wordsworth's prose.

reference to the powers of mind *predominant* in the production of them."[2] These two topics are the core of his most formal statement of his poetic doctrine, the Preface to the edition of 1815. During the intervening century and a half Wordsworth's system of classification and his attempts to define the two most important terms of his criticism have been ridiculed, ignored, and defended—but never really explained. Even Arthur Beatty's spirited and well-documented defense of the classifications regularly abandons the critical issues raised in the Preface of 1815 for more detailed discussion of its far better known predecessor, the Preface to *Lyrical Ballads*.[3]

The main purpose of this study is to exhibit in a selection from Wordsworth's poetry the evidence of his preoccupation with the roles of imagination and fancy in the composition of poetry and his concern with the manner in which a psychologically valid classification and arrangement of apparently miscellaneous poems can "serve as a commentary unostentatiously directing [the reader's] attention" so as to produce responses predetermined by the poet.[4] These topics have been anything but ignored through decades of Wordsworthian criticism, yet for some reason there has been no systematic application of the principles of Wordsworth's classification and arrangement to the poems

[2] *PW*, II, 433.

[3] Arthur Beatty, *William Wordsworth: His Doctrine and Art in their Historical Relations* (3rd ed.; Madison: University of Wisconsin Press, 1960). It is largely because of Beatty's study that the Preface to *Lyrical Ballads* became so well known. The reader familiar with his comments on fancy and imagination and on Wordsworth's system of arranging his poems will recognize our points of disagreement.

[4] *PW*, II, 434.

that he gathered under the headings "Poems of the Fancy" and "Poems of the Imagination" in editions that he himself supervised. Such an examination is the principal object of this study.

Its title is also the title of a popular poetry anthology edited by Leigh Hunt and published in 1844. In the earlier *Imagination and Fancy*, subtitled *Selections from the English Poets*, one looks in vain for a poem by Wordsworth or any mention of him. Hunt's explanation, stated in his preface, that "for obvious reasons no living writer is included," does not obscure the irony that a book bearing such a title, published at such a time, should take no note whatsoever of the influence of Wordsworth and Coleridge in establishing the imagination as the definitive test of poetic value.[5]

Hunt's own definitions of imagination and fancy are instructive historically but not absolutely: imagination is that faculty by means of which a poem "embodies and illustrates its impressions," while fancy, presumably incapable of embodying, merely illustrates impressions. Fancy is "a lighter play of imagination, or the feeling of analogy coming short of seriousness, in order that it may laugh with what it loves, and show how it can decorate it with fairy ornament" (p. 2). Coleridge (along with Hunt's friend Keats) is cited as a poet chiefly of fancy, in contrast to Homer and Dante, poets of imagination; Shakespeare, predictably, is granted supreme excellence in both faculties. It is difficult to judge from so brief a catalogue, but Hunt seems inclined to place imagination in the distant past, thus

[5] Leigh Hunt, ed., *Imagination and Fancy; or Selections from the English Poets* (American ed.; New York, 1850), p. ix.

3

depriving the Romantic movement of its principal article of faith.[6]

Even if Wordsworth had been among the eligible dead when Hunt was making his selections, it is unlikely that his work would have been generously represented, if represented at all. Apart from possible extraneous considerations, it would not have met Hunt's most important criterion for inclusion, for he deliberately limited the anthology to *"poetry of the most poetical kind*, or such as exhibits the imagination and fancy in a state of predominance, undisputed by interests of another sort. . . . [poetry] in its element, like an essence distilled" (p. viii). The subject here is "pure" poetry, and in time and spirit Hunt's notion of the most poetical poetry is very close to Poe's.[7]

[6] If, that is, one can assume that Hunt's parallelism is consistent. The relevant passage reads as follows: "It [poetry] varies . . . from the most tremendous to the most playful effusions, and from imagination to fancy through all their degrees;—from Homer and Dante, to Coleridge and Keats;—from Shakespeare in King Lear, to Shakespeare himself in the Midsummer Night's Dream; from Spenser's Faerie Queene, to the Castle of Indolence . . ." (pp. viii–ix).

[7] Although Hunt's remarks are far from self-consistent, there are hints that despite his subordination of fancy to imagination in the preface, he responds with more natural affection to what he considers to be products of fancy. Especially in his comments on Spenser and Keats, he all but identifies fancy as the faculty of "pure" poetry (pp. 50–51, 230–231). If so his remarks constitute a (probably unconscious) repudiation of the poetic values of both Coleridge and Wordsworth, and not merely what Meyer H. Abrams calls a "degeneration of Coleridge's distinction." See *The Mirror and the Lamp* (New York: W. W. Norton and Company, 1958), p. 182. But Hunt's comments on the terms inspire no confidence. He can, for example, assert that Coleridge has "little fancy, but imagination exquisite" (p. 23); later on say that Coleridge's verse abounds in sweetness, "the smoothness of grace and delicacy" (p. 29); and then praise Shakespeare's fancy for these same qualities that Coleridge, who has "little fancy," shares with Shakespeare (p. 106).

4

Poetic taste in Hunt's criticism is narrowed to an appreciation for the lyric or for lyrical parts of non-lyric poems, and imagination and fancy are little more than useful badges of relative merit. Yet even in his rather casual approach to these terms, Hunt evinces more interest in distinguishing between them than did more famous contemporary poets. Byron, Shelley, and Keats, the sometimes unwilling heirs to the Wordsworth-Coleridge tradition, displayed varying degrees of unconcern for distinctions between poetic faculties. Modern critics still find the term *imagination* useful, but the distinction between fancy and imagination seems either factitious or impossible to make precisely.[8] To Coleridge and Wordsworth, however, this distinction was a matter of urgent, even vital importance.

[8] From Wordsworth's time to ours this view of his distinction has prevailed. Professor Shawcross agrees with Sara Coleridge, who "was perhaps the first to point out [that] many of the poems classed by Wordsworth under the heading 'Poems of the Fancy' are by no means distinguished chiefly by this characteristic." Coleridge, *Biographia Literaria*, ed. J. Shawcross (rev. ed.; London: Oxford University Press, 1962), II, 293; hereafter cited as *BL*. R. D. Havens quotes this note by Shawcross and endorses it. See *The Mind of a Poet* (Baltimore: Johns Hopkins Press, 1941), p. 465. A notable exception to the neglect of Wordsworth's distinction among modern poets is Wallace Stevens. See "The Noble Rider and the Sound of Words," in *The Necessary Angel* (New York: Alfred A. Knopf, 1951), pp. 10–11.

I

The Two Wordsworths

Because in Wordsworth's poetry everything is related to everything else, his conception of the differences between imagination and fancy and the arrangement of his miscellaneous poems have guaranteed relevance. They deserve a prominent place, for example, in discussions of that most venerable of topics, the decline of his poetic powers.

Whatever names are given to Wordsworth's poetic voices, it is generally agreed that there are radically different styles in his poetry. Most modern critics have reduced their number to two, usually called "Romantic" and "Neoclassical," and this practice is at least partially confirmed by Wordsworth's belief in the existence of two distinct poetic faculties, with purposes and modes of expression appropriate to each. In quite simple terms—admittedly, too simple to stand without qualification— imagination is the faculty of Wordsworth's Romantic mode, fancy, of his Neo-classical or traditional styles and forms of expression.[1]

[1] A number of modern scholars have advanced our understanding of fundamental differences in metaphysics and style between Romantic poetry and that of earlier periods. A few citations must stand for many: Meyer H. Abrams, *The Mirror and the Lamp* (New York: W. W. Norton and Company, 1958); Frank Kermode, *Romantic*

To learn more about Wordsworth's understanding of these faculties should help to put into clearer perspective that probably futile but fascinating question of whether there are two Wordsworths. It helps to know, for example, that Wordsworth's adherence to these two poetic styles was not successive. Even during his greatest period of creativity, he was employing the same techniques of explicit statement and conventional imagery that characterize the poems of his decline. The later poetry merely exhibits in exaggerated form tendencies already established in the early poems of fancy.

Wordsworth's simultaneous use of the two modes of expression subsumed under the labels *fancy* and *imagination* reflects not only his own indecision but that uncertainty which always attends a transitional period. The world into which Wordsworth was born in 1770 shifted its glance nervously from past to future, and through all of Wordsworth's formative years his generation regularly transferred its faith and its loyalties between discredited beliefs of the past and the undefined outlines of some future system of values. Wordsworth shared with his thoughtful contemporaries a commitment divided between two sets of

---

Image (London: Routledge and Kegan Paul Ltd., 1957); Josephine Miles, *Eras and Modes in English Poetry* (Berkeley and Los Angeles: University of California Press, 1957); Morse Peckham, "Toward a Theory of Romanticism," *PMLA*, LXVI (1951), 5–23, and "Toward a Theory of Romanticism: II. Reconsiderations," *Studies In Romanticism*, I, 1961), 1–8; Earl R. Wasserman, *The Subtler Language* (Baltimore: Johns Hopkins Press, 1959); Basil Willey, "Wordsworth and the Locke Tradition," in *The Seventeenth Century Background* (New York: Columbia University Press, 1952). A major influence on recent reassessments of poetic symbolism is Susanne K. Langer's *Philosophy in a New Key* (2nd ed.; Cambridge: Harvard University Press, 1951).

assumptions about the relationship between man and the external world that today continue to wage their indecisive struggle. By Wordsworth's time this conflict had become further complicated by a tendency to fuse aesthetics with morals and metaphysics, so that artistic problems assumed an importance and scope never before and never since known. From the melancholy perspective of our century, the Romantic period is seen as a brief apotheosis of poetry that was the prelude to what now seems its permanent banishment from the stage of man's daily life and most persistent concerns.

Wordsworth was the first forthright spokesman for a new kind of poetry that challenged science for the right to discover and to proclaim truths. His manifesto, the Preface to *Lyrical Ballads*, was designed to enunciate a poetic doctrine that was expressly opposed to the two attitudes toward poetry prevailing at the end of the eighteenth century. According to one of these attitudes, poetry was to draw upon and to illustrate a body of concepts discovered by the senses and rational faculties, the "facts" of the man of science. This attitude, Wordsworth believed, was the basis for the poetry of Dryden, Pope, and their followers.[2] The second of these attitudes, even more demeaning to poetry, was represented chiefly by Erasmus Darwin, who spun fanciful worlds that have no illuminating relationship

[2] For Wordsworth's implied distinction between fact and truth, see his discussion of the poet and the man of science in the Preface to *Lyrical Ballads*, *PW*, II, 394–397; and James Scoggins, "The Preface to *Lyrical Ballads*: A Revolution in Dispute," in *Studies in Criticism and Aesthetics, 1660–1800*, ed. Howard A. Anderson and John S. Shea (Minneapolis: University of Minnesota Press, 1966). See also Basil Willey's contrast between the poetry of Wordsworth and James Thomson, in *The Seventeenth Century Background*, pp. 295–296.

to the real one. The principal intention of the Preface and the poems of *Lyrical Ballads* was to expound and to embody the doctrine that the highest kind of poetry yields insights into reality transcending the powers of sense and the understanding. Although Wordsworth himself sometimes speaks as if his poetic doctrine were simply a return to critical theories antedating the English Restoration, it is in fact as alien to the Renaissance as to the Neo-classical period.

Those poems of the Great Decade that Wordsworth attributed to imagination are the fruits of this new doctrine. But Wordsworth, the only Romantic poet to whom this doctrine was also a religious faith, could not escape entirely the older conceptions of poetry. Most of the poems of fancy bear the stamp of his individual genius, but they are closer, both in style and spirit, to eighteenth-century nature poetry than to his own poems of imagination. Whether in a playful or a serious mood, Wordsworth's fancy either illustrates previously accepted interpretations of reality or ignores reality in order to substitute charming "fanciful" creations.

The presence of three such different attitudes in his poetry helps to account for Wordsworth's debts to such diverse patterns of thought as British empiricism and German transcendentalism. To recall, moreover, the great influence of the first of these traditions on the second prepares the reader of Wordsworth's prose for its mixture of Neo-classical and Romantic assumptions and vocabulary.

Wordsworth's election into the company of great poets is an accomplished fact. But his election was by no means unanimous, and his rank among poets remains a debatable issue. His genius never has been, and probably never will be acknowledged with that near-absence of reservation that characterizes the status of other great English poets. Even in these waning years of the reaction against romanticism, one feels that of the undeniably major poets Wordsworth is the most vulnerable. One risks rather little in declaring himself a skeptic toward Wordsworth's achievement, and one can so declare himself even in a volume commemorating the poet's death.[3]

The reasons for some modern critics' coolness toward Wordsworth are not distinctly modern reasons. They existed in 1798 and were stated with special vigor when Wordsworth gave fullest expression to his thoughts on poetry in the Preface to the edition of 1815 and in his organization of the poems of these volumes. One of these reasons is particularly vexing: critics expect that great poetry will be complex, but for years the virtue of Wordsworth's poetry most often cited is its simplicity. An enigmatic yet helpful formulation of what might be called the Wordsworthian paradox is the following observation by Helen Darbishire: "Unlike most modern poets Wordsworth requires no commentary: his style is simple and lucid, his subject matter in no way exotic. Yet what he has to say is by no means obvious, by no means easily understood."[4]

[3] Douglas Bush, "Wordsworth: A Minority Report," in *Wordsworth: Centenary Studies*, ed. Gilbert T. Dunklin (Princeton: Princeton University Press, 1951), pp. 3–22. Bush's skepticism is softened by his many generous remarks about Wordsworth and by his unfailing good manners.

[4] Helen Darbishire, "Wordsworth's Significance for Us," in *The Major English Romantic Poets*, ed. Clarence D. Thorpe, Carlos Baker, and Bennett Weaver (Carbondale: Southern Illinois University Press, 1957), p. 74. Cf. Howard Nemerov on the poetry of Wallace Stevens, in whom Nemerov can sometimes "catch some usually tenuous hint of kinship" with Wordsworth: ". . . the difficulty of

If Wordsworth's poetry requires no commentary (in the refined sense that term has acquired in modern criticism), it most certainly requires a context. An important part of that context, embodied in Wordsworth's classification and arrangement of his poems, has not been accorded a sufficiently sympathetic hearing.

---

these poems, which have about them an 'impenetrable lucidity,' a brilliance of surface that defeats sometimes the kind of explication that works tolerably well on a good deal of English poetry. That is, we are sometimes compelled to wish a little wistfully for a moment requiring esoteric knowledge, as with Eliot, or the sorting-out of syntax or complex metaphor, as with Donne, Yeats, and a number of others; but Stevens is most difficult at precisely the moments of greatest simplicity . . . ." Howard Nemerov, "The Poetry of Wallace Stevens," in *Poetry and Fiction: Essays* (New Brunswick: Rutgers University Press, 1963), pp. 75, 76–77.

2

Wordsworth and Philosophy

From Coleridge to Matthew Arnold critics and reviewers of Wordsworth's poetry identified certain impediments to a just appreciation of it. Some of these criticisms have been all but forgotten, but a few remain with us today. One is Wordsworth's sometimes embarrassing simplicity of subject and expression, for while simplicity is almost always a word of praise when applied to his poetry, many readers have felt that the line between simplicity and triviality is not always comfortably distinguishable. And then, as Arnold rather plaintively remarked, there is the dispiriting bulk and unevenness of Wordsworth's poetry and the delusion, shared, Arnold feared, by Wordsworth himself, that he was a "philosophic" poet. Arnold tried to eliminate these last two obstacles between Wordsworth and his readers by selecting for his edition of Wordsworth only those poems likely to revive the poet's former reputation and popularity.[1]

Swayed probably more than he knew by a fad for "pure" poetry (to which Hunt's anthology is another monument), Arnold presented to his readers a Wordsworth distilled to his lyric essence. In this way he was able to avoid a rivalry

[1] Matthew Arnold, Preface to *Poems of Wordsworth* (London, 1879).

between his two modern poetic idols, Wordsworth and Goethe. Evincing here, as elsewhere, a protective attitude toward his friend and countryman, Arnold withdrew Wordsworth from any possible competition with the truly philosophic poet of the Romantic period, and attempted to enshrine him as the perfect complement to Goethe—the German's intellectual vigor and sophistication would provide one noble kind of spiritual inspiration, Wordsworth's childlike lyricism and naïveté, another.

One need not accept Coleridge's exaggerated notion of Wordsworth's poetic mission to sense that Arnold sacrificed an important element of Wordsworth's genius. In fact Arnold's interpretation of Wordsworth demonstrates the power of will over reason. Needing desperately a poet free from the trammels of doubt and despair, he demanded and got from Wordsworth the antidote to his own disease of spirit. In the process he condemned Wordsworthian criticism to decades of attempts to settle Wordsworth's status as a philosopher. Finally that quest appears to have taken a more profitable direction, and the trend of recent criticism has been toward demonstrating precisely the elements of Wordsworth's faith (or faiths) that made an impact on his poetry.[2]

[2] The word *philosophic* has, after all, both precise and enormously general meanings. When applied to a poet, it can be merely a way of saying that he is very serious about his art and that his interest extends to matters not strictly aesthetic. But Wordsworth was a philosophic poet in a wider sense than this. Geoffrey H. Hartman can remark that in *The Prelude* Wordsworth's "mild *anima mundi* mysticism" and "secondhand Spinozism . . . provide a quasi-philosophical dignity for his view of nature," and then, quite correctly, use philosophic concepts and terminology to analyze Wordsworth's poetry. See *Wordsworth's Poetry, 1787–1814* (New Haven and London: Yale University Press, 1964), p. 193. I regret that Hartman's important book appeared after the present study was written.

The history of Wordsworth's reputation has not, but should have been, the history of critical attitudes toward the system of organization that he devised so carefully for editions of his poems. None of Wordsworth's activities as a poet is a more certain indication of the serious purpose that he claimed for his poetry, and none is more distinctively Wordsworthian. Arnold's attitude toward this effort is symptomatic of his vision of Wordsworth's poetry, and this is a vision by no means defunct:

> Wordsworth classified his poems not according to any commonly received plan of arrangement, but according to a scheme of mental physiology.... His categories are ingenious but far-fetched, and the result of his employment of them is unsatisfactory. Poems are separated one from another which possess a kinship of subject or of treatment far more vital and deep than the supposed unity of mental origin which was Wordsworth's reason for joining them with others.... Wordsworth's poems will never produce their due effect until they are freed from their present artificial arrangement, and grouped more naturally.[3]

Arnold was not the first to express dissatisfaction with Wordsworth's organizing principles. From the moment they were enunciated in the Preface of 1815, even the admirers of Wordsworth's poems found little to praise in his classification and arrangement of them. Despite Wordsworth's several attempts to explain to him the reasons behind this system, his friend Henry Crabb Robinson continued to believe that at best it was hardly worth the poet's efforts. Robinson was perhaps the most faithful of Wordsworth's advocates, but he found fault not only with

[3] Arnold, Preface to *Poems of Wordsworth*, xii–xiii.

15

the organization of the poems but with the Preface. He thought it "subtle," but "not clear or intelligible," and he objected to the classifications used by Wordsworth on the grounds that they are "partly subjective and partly objective."[4]

Most subsequent commentators have experienced Robinson's confusion and doubt, but few have shown his earnest desire to understand that which he was criticizing. The following remarks from *The Monthly Review* of 1815 are, unhappily, not exceptional, either in substance or in tone: ". . . in the present volumes [of the edition of 1815] we have a poem belonging to the class of 'Fancy,' with no possible distinguishing characteristic from another in the class of 'Imagination'. . . . in short, we have here . . . a pompous classification of trifles, for the most part obvious and extremely childish . . . ."[5] The tenor and temper of these comments have echoed through modern estimations of Wordsworth's arrangement.[6]

Given the general unpopularity of Wordsworth's system of organization, his editors have faced a difficult decision. Of all scholars, a good editor is most aware of his responsibilities to the writer whose works he makes available to the public, yet he owes to that public another obligation

---

[4] *Henry Crabb Robinson on Books and their Writers*, ed. Edith J. Morley (London: J. M. Dent and Sons Ltd., 1938), I, 165.

[5] *The Monthly Review*, LXXVIII (1815), 226.

[6] See, e.g., George McLean Harper, *William Wordsworth: His Life, Works, and Influence* (New York: Charles Scribner's Sons, 1916), II, 251; Herbert Read, *Wordsworth* (London: Jonathan Cape, 1930), pp. 161–162; F. R. Leavis, *Revaluation* (London: Chatto and Windus, 1962), p. 158. In, of all places, Wordsworth's own *Memoirs*, edited by Christopher Wordsworth, there is the terse remark that the "poems to be studied profitably should be read chronologically" (London, 1851, I, 4).

sometimes in conflict with the first: to present the works that he edits in the way most likely to benefit his readers. Since Wordsworth believed so intensely in his own system of organization, his editors have been confronted with a decision that is less editorial than philosophic. Not surprisingly, their responses to this dilemma have varied.

The editor of the first major complete edition of Wordsworth's poetry was William Knight. In preparing his edition, Knight chose to substitute for the arrangement in editions supervised by Wordsworth a chronological arrangement by order of composition. He respected Wordsworth's own wishes, even admitting that "almost any author would attach more importance to a classification of his works, which brought them together under appropriate headings irrespective of date, than to a method of arrangement which exhibited the growth of his own mind." Yet it was precisely because of his desire to exhibit the growth of the poet's mind that Knight decided upon a chronological arrangement, the same one that Charles Lamb had suggested and that Wordsworth had rejected as "the very worst that could be followed."[7]

Despite the great influence of Arnold's preface to his selection of Wordsworth's poetry and Knight's edition, later editors—notably Dowden, Hutchinson, and De Selincourt—refused to substitute their principles of arrangement for Wordsworth's. The happy result of their deference is that the best editions of the poems have employed the plan that Wordsworth thought best, not necessarily because

[7] William Knight, Preface to *The Poetical Works of William Wordsworth* (Edinburgh, 1882–1886), I, xi. Wordsworth's rebuff of Lamb's suggestion is recorded in *The Correspondence of Henry Crabb Robinson with the Wordsworth Circle*, ed. Edith J. Morley (Oxford: Oxford University Press, 1927), I, 164.

the editors were themselves convinced of its value, but because, in Dowden's words, they felt that "it would be doing violence to his intentions to adopt any other order for the poems than that devised thoughtfully and deliberately by himself."[8]

Of the men who prepared the three major editions of the Poetical Works, only Dowden seems really to have understood Wordsworth's principles of arrangement and his preface contains the earliest lucid discussion of them:

> Whether the classification be happy or not, it should be borne in mind, first, that the psychological groups [Fancy, Imagination, etc.] form only part of a larger design, and secondly, that the order of the poems *within each group* is Wordsworth's order, and that it was carefully considered with a view to artistic effect.... the poems move in order, bound to each other by a continuous though unapparent tie. The succession of poems does not form a cast-iron series of links, but rather a wreath of flowers lightly entwined with one another. (I, ix–x)

Dowden supports his general description with a skillful illustration of the arrangement of poems grouped under the headings "Poems Founded on the Affections" and "Miscellaneous Sonnets." His demonstration is both judicious and convincing, but, regrettably, it is also very brief. Were it not for this, it is unlikely that Wordsworth's arrangement would require today either an explanation or a defense.

But with the exception of Dowden, Wordsworth's modern editors have either rejected his plan of arrangement or accepted it with obvious reluctance. John Morley, for example, followed Knight's lead in organizing the poems in order of composition, and by this time, 1888, felt no need

[8] Edward Dowden, Preface to *The Poetical Works of William Wordsworth* (London, 1892–1893), I, viii.

to defend this procedure.[9] In 1895, however, Thomas Hutchinson presented what is still the best one-volume edition of the poems, and retained Wordsworth's arrangement. Like his dating of the poems and his establishing of their texts, Hutchinson's discussion of this arrangement is responsibly cautious: "On this question of arrangement, the Editor is fain to confess, his affections are most humble; he has no ambition to see a goodlier scheme than Wordsworth's. . . . As to the advantages alleged by some to accompany a chronological arrangement of the poems, it will be time enough to discuss them when the materials for the construction of such an arrangement are in our hands."[10] Hutchinson's last remark was surely directed at Knight's edition. The opportunity to study the growth of the poet's mind that Knight claimed for his arrangement was not really possible until sufficient evidence was uncovered to fix dates of composition more accurately.

Ernest de Selincourt, to whom much more of this evidence was available, believed that an arrangement according to dates of composition is worse than a simple arrangement according to publication dates. In addition to Wordsworth's strong feelings against this method of organization, De Selincourt raised the objection that such an arrangement "separates poems that are by nature joined together and belong to one another, and substitutes for an essential kinship of thought and feeling an accidental and often irrelevant order in time, which registers indiscriminately the exalted and more trivial moods." Despite this eloquent support of Wordsworth's principles and his

[9] John Morley, ed., *The Complete Poetical Works of William Wordsworth* (London, 1888).
[10] Thomas Hutchinson, Preface to *The Poetical Works of Wordsworth* (London: Oxford University Press, 1932), p. ix.

adoption of Wordsworth's arrangement for his definitive edition, De Selincourt was far from convinced of the plan's soundness. His decision to adopt it resulted not from conviction, but from the serious weaknesses inherent in all alternative arrangements. Criticism of Wordsworth's system, he admits, "is easy enough," and his objections to it merit careful consideration: ". . . it will not stand logical examination. In part psychological . . . in part by form . . . it is, in fact, a compromise. The divisions are not mutually exclusive, but overlap; Wordsworth, indeed, himself showed uncertainty as to the rightful position of some of the poems, shifting them in successive editions from class to class."[11] De Selincourt's criticism is unquestionably just. The arrangement is a compromise, classes do overlap, and Wordsworth did have difficulty in applying his classifications to particular poems. But these inconsistencies and difficulties were not enough to dissuade Wordsworth from persisting in his method of organization, and they should not dissuade those who wish to understand that persistence.

From its first appearance to the present time, Wordsworth's arrangement has produced many critics and few defenders. It has, however, found in addition to Dowden two very articulate champions, separated by almost a century but united in their faith that Wordsworth's arrangement has advantages over all others. The first of these was Wordsworth's American editor, Professor Henry Reed of Philadelphia. Reed was the first editor to put to practical use the principles of this arrangement, when in preparing a one-volume edition of the poems in 1837, he faced the problem of integrating poems published by Wordsworth in 1835 (*Yarrow Revisited and other Poems*)

[11] *PW*, I, ix–x.

with the poet's complete edition of 1832 in such a way as to arrange the whole in harmony with Wordsworth's principles of organization. In his totally unqualified enthusiasm for these principles Reed is unique among Wordsworth's editors. To publish the *Yarrow* poems as a separate group, he wrote, "would have betrayed an ignorance or distrust of [Wordsworth's] principles of classification, or a timidity in applying them. It would have been a method purely mechanical, and calculated to impair the effect of that philosophical arrangement...."[12] Instead, Reed arranged the poems according to his understanding of Wordsworth's principles.

As might be expected, Reed's success in this undertaking was limited; his classifications and his ordering of poems did not correspond exactly with those of Wordsworth's own fifth edition, published in 1836–1837. But however he differed with Wordsworth's own subsequent placement of some poems, Reed was confident that Wordsworth's principles of organization are both valid and discernible. There is reason to doubt, however, that he really understood Wordsworth's system, particularly his classifying of poems, as well as he thought he did. Near the end of his preface he makes this curious statement: "Pains have been taken to indicate typographically, in a manner more clear than in any former edition, the general classification of the Poems" (p. iv). A look at Reed's edition discloses that his typographical alteration consists of applying the heading "Poems of the Imagination" to poems that had not been included in this classification in editions that Wordsworth had supervised. Thus, in Reed's edition the following

[12] Henry Reed, Preface to *The Complete Poetical Works of William Wordsworth* (Philadelphia, 1837), p. iii.

21

additional groups of poems are included under this heading: "Miscellaneous Sonnets," "Memorials of a Tour in Scotland, 1803," "Memorials of a Tour in Scotland, 1814," "Sonnets Dedicated to Liberty," "Memorials of a Tour on the Continent, 1820," "The River Duddon," "Sonnets Composed . . . during a Tour in Scotland . . . in 1833," "The White Doe of Rylstone," and "Ecclesiastical Sketches." His reason for thus extending the classification "Poems of the Imagination" is not stated, but presumably it was his desire to correct the inconsistency in Wordsworth's scheme to which De Selincourt later called attention, the confusion of psychological with other bases for classification. That Reed's naïve solution found favor with Wordsworth is a matter to which I shall return.

Arthur Beatty, the most recent advocate of Wordsworth's arrangement, applauded Reed's expansion of the category "Poems of the Imagination" as a clarification of Wordsworth's intentions and regretted "that modern editors have not conformed to Wordsworth's own interpretation and application of the term [imagination]" by adopting Reed's alteration, which Wordsworth himself adopted in the one-volume edition he prepared for publication in 1845. This alteration seemed a decided improvement to Beatty, whose thesis is that Wordsworth identifies fancy as the immature and imagination as the mature mental faculty, and who therefore thought it proper that Wordsworth should attribute to the imagination all poems "which were not expressly excluded as being more strongly marked by subject-matter or by form."[13]

[13] Arthur Beatty, *William Wordsworth: His Doctrine and Art in their Historical Relations* (3rd ed.; Madison: University of Wisconsin Press, 1960), pp. 201–203.

Despite the great influence of Beatty's publications, the prevailing view of Wordsworth's system of organization is substantially the same as the view prevailing in 1815, that, as James V. Logan puts it, the classifications are "confusing and inexact," and "it is . . . difficult to distinguish between poems placed in the class of 'Imagination' and those under the head of 'Fancy.'"[14]

Most writers who have commented on the edition of 1815 have been less critical of Wordsworth's arrangement of the poems than of his classification of two groups of them as poems owing their composition principally to either fancy or imagination, and of his attempts in the Preface to describe the operations of these faculties. Immediately after the appearance of reviews of that edition, most of Wordsworth's critics, friendly and unfriendly alike, returned, apparently with a feeling of relief, to the revised Preface to *Lyrical Ballads*. This turn of events could hardly have pleased Wordsworth, for beginning with the edition of 1815 he relegated that Preface to the end of the last volume of his poems.

The terms *imagination* and *fancy* have long outlasted Wordsworth, but at great cost. Today, for most who use them at all, they have become, respectively, merely vaguely honorific and slightly pejorative labels, or a means of distinguishing between poems of high seriousness and playful, pretty verse. This development is bad enough, but there is one even worse, the habit of looking to Coleridge for explanations of Wordsworth's distinction between these faculties. The practice began even before the publication

[14] James V. Logan, *Wordsworthian Criticism* (Columbus: Ohio State University Press, 1947), p. 74.

23

of the *Biographia Literaria*. In December, 1816, Crabb Robinson wrote that "Wordsworth's obscure discrimination between fancy and imagination in his last preface is greatly illustrated by what Coleridge has here [in his *Lay Sermons*] said and written."[15] But Robinson was wrong. What he thought was illustration was a false light that obscured rather than illuminated Wordsworth's distinction. It may be true that "from Coleridge's point of view, Wordsworth's vocabulary [in the Preface of 1815] showed a regressive tendency to conflate the organic imagination with mechanical fancy," but the point of view implied in the terminology of this judgment is not one to which Wordsworth would have acceded.[16]

It would be folly to argue that Wordsworth was a more philosophic thinker than Coleridge, and it may be true that even the truncated descriptions of imagination and fancy in the *Biographia* are more lucid, more self-consistent, and more respectably philosophical than Wordsworth's own.[17] But it is Wordsworth's conceptions that produced his plan for arranging his poems, and his conceptions that can illuminate the arrangement and its principles. And if these are to be understood, they must be considered not as misapplications of Coleridge's distinction between the two faculties, but as the results of another distinction entirely, no less important in its points of disagreement than in its points of agreement with that of Coleridge.

[15] Morley, *Henry Crabb Robinson*, I, 200.

[16] Meyer H. Abrams, *The Mirror and the Lamp* (New York: W. W. Norton and Company, 1958), p. 181. For Wordsworth's refusal to accept Coleridge's characterization of fancy, see *PW*, II, 440–441.

[17] *BL*, I, 60–65, 195–202.

3

Toward the Edition of 1815

⟨————⟩

Wordsworth's need for "a theme / Single and of determined bounds" was important not only in the genesis of *The Prelude*, but in his conception of his poems as a whole.[1] A distinctive characteristic of most English poetry written prior to the Romantic period is its adaptability to a variety of occasions and purposes. Conversely, a major feature of Romantic and of modern poetry is the authors' concern that their separate poems produce a totality of effect, with the continuity and internal relevance that such a design implies. It is true that there is something of this tendency in the sonnet cycle and in series of eclogues, and more in the conception of lesser genres as steps toward the epic. Still, as with most such tendencies, the difference between Romantic and ante-Romantic manifestations of them is the greater degree of conscious (and self-conscious) intent in the Romantic poets.

From the very beginning of his maturity as a poet, Wordsworth thought of his individual poems as parts of a

[1] *The Prelude*, ed. Ernest de Selincourt and Helen Darbishire (2nd ed.; Oxford: Oxford University Press, 1959), I, 640–641. All quotations are taken from this edition, and, unless an earlier version is indicated, follow the 1850 text; hereafter cited as *Prelude*.

single grand design. Thanks to almost a century of attempts to devise an alternative to rigorously Neo-classical aesthetic principles, he had available to him when he came to announce this design an image that could express precisely what he called his "two-fold view" of his poems, their interdependence as parts of a whole, yet their individual integrity as works of art complete in themselves.[2] This image, the Gothic church, had the additional merits of suggesting to Wordsworth the kinship of poetry and the religious sublime and of invalidating as standards of judgment the strict demands for proportion and balance of an earlier taste.[3] Like Gothic architecture, Wordsworth's poems were to be judged according to the spirit rather than the letter and were to appeal to faculties more closely allied to religious than to purely aesthetic sensibilities. His criticism and his best poems owe much of their uniqueness to this conception of poetry and of the relationships among his poems. For if each poem is profoundly affected by every other, a body of poems can express a living, growing personality and in this way imitate the vital unity of organic Nature. The poet, then, in the act of creation becomes "A power like one of Nature's" (*Prelude*, XIII, 312).

Wordsworth's conception of the organic unity of his apparently miscellaneous poems existed at least as early as

[2] Preface of 1815, *PW*, II, 434.

[3] This image appears in Wordsworth's first formal statement of the relationships among his poems, the Preface to the 1814 edition of *The Excursion*, wherein the miscellaneous or "minor Pieces" are likened to "the little cells, oratories, and sepulchral recesses" of the church, and *The Prelude* to its "ante-chapel" (*PW*, V, 2). Perhaps an analogy drawn from living things would have better suited his organic theory, but Wordsworth was apparently less concerned with consistency of imagery than with the religious implications of his analogy.

1798. In that year Coleridge wrote to the first printer of *Lyrical Ballads*, Joseph Cottle, that Cottle's plan to publish some of the poems "singly" was to Wordsworth "decisively repugnant & oppugnant," because both poets considered "that the volumes offered to you are to a certain degree *one work*, in *kind tho' not in degree*, as an Ode is one work—& that our different poems are as stanzas, good relatively rather than absolutely."[4] The modern reader would likely only pause to nod agreement with Coleridge's explanation and not question at all the assumptions underlying it, but if Cottle was not a bit surprised he was far ahead of his time.

The first edition of *Lyrical Ballads* gives little apparent evidence of Wordsworth's desire to organize his poems. The title page does list two groups, lyrical ballads and "a few other poems," but these are hardly distinct classifications.[5] In the arrangement of poems some attention is paid to placing together those of obviously related subjects or themes, but this much awareness of relationships among poems could be expected even from a poet not expressly interested in a pattern of organization.[6] It is doubtful that Wordsworth's great desire to arrange his poems systematically could be inferred from the first edition alone, but the

[4] *Collected Letters of Samuel Taylor Coleridge*, ed. Earl Leslie Griggs (Oxford: Oxford University Press, 1956–1959), I, 411–412.

[5] Arthur Beatty, however, saw in the two groups on the title page the germ of Wordsworth's later classifications. *William Wordsworth: His Doctrine and Art in their Historical Relations* (3rd ed.; Madison: University of Wisconsin Press, 1960), p. 196.

[6] Obviously complementary poems ("Anecdote for Fathers" and "We Are Seven," "Expostulation and Reply" and "The Tables Turned") are linked, and, with more hint of careful design, so are two poems on maternal love ("The Mad Mother" and "The Idiot Boy") and three on human suffering ("Old Man Travelling," "The Complaint of the Forsaken Indian Woman," and "The Convict").

organization of the expanded second edition of 1800 puts the matter beyond inference. While the two volumes of this edition were being prepared, Wordsworth wrote to the printers Biggs and Cottle his instructions to "print this poem ["Michael"] immediately after the 'Poems on the Naming of Places,'" and added this injunction: "If it does not fill up so much space as to make the [second] volume 205 pages, you must not immediately print the Poem of *Michael*, as I wish it to conclude the volume."[7]

The classification of one group of poems as "Poems on the Naming of Places" seems casual enough, but it was a large step toward the elaborate classification of poems in the first collected edition, published in 1815. The principal concern of his organization of the volumes of 1800 was not, however, with classification but with arrangement. The first of the two volumes contains poems reprinted from the first edition, but these are extensively and carefully rearranged.[8] The poems in this volume form seven groups, and the unifying theme is the power of the sympathetic imagination, which both Coleridge and Wordsworth proposed as a cure for the two prominent maladies of their age, an excessive reliance on the purely rational faculties and the unhealthy indulgence of a flaccid sentimentality. Each poem and each group of poems expounds or illustrates this major theme. Fortunately, the great variety of styles and forms devoted to the theme permits it to emerge distinctly but subtly, so that while a few poems are very

[7] *Early Letters of William and Dorothy Wordsworth*, ed. Ernest de Selincourt (Oxford: Oxford University Press, 1935), p. 257; hereafter cited as *EL*.

[8] Both arrangements appear in Appendix A, pp. 229–231.

close to being obviously "program" pieces, the volume as a whole escapes this fate.[9]

The first group is composed of three poems; the first two, "Expostulation and Reply" and "The Tables Turned," expound, and the third, "Animal Tranquillity and Decay" (entitled "Old Man Travelling" in 1798), dramatizes the value of "wise passiveness" as a means of receiving from Nature sensations that can become the basis for moral principles more distinctly human (hence more humane) than those devised by the cold intellect.[10] The last poem of this group, its subject being the sufferings of a father who has lost his son, provides a link to the next group, poems four through seven.

The poems of this group are all "complaints" arising from various kinds of loss. The speaker in the first one, "The Complaint of a Forsaken Indian Woman" demonstrates the superior strength of emotional to rational processes. Her excited imagination moves her mind from practical assessments of her desperate situation to pleas for a quick death that conflict with her instinct for survival. Even that most elementary of instincts is subordinated in the woman's mind and in the theme of the poem to the potency of maternal affection. As the poem unfolds by dramatic progression, we witness a mysterious process by which possession of the child and its absence from her become,

[9] The theme I describe might be said to apply to the second volume of 1800 as well, or for that matter to most of Wordsworth's poems, but it is more pronounced and nearer the surface in volume one of 1800 than in any other volume.

[10] I cannot accept the popular notion that the first two poems are little more than *jeux d'esprit*. On the attitude complementing wise passiveness see pp. 98, 203, 225–226.

respectively, imaginative equivalents of life and death. This natural symbolism, vested in the imagination, is the mind's way of assimilating the external world into itself.[11]

The other three poems dramatize more directly the superiority of natural to what might be called artificial learning. In various ways all three poems emphasize the fundamental limitations and dangers involved in knowledge of this second sort. If "true knowledge leads to love," the obvious implication is that false—that is, "unnatural"— knowledge leads to something that is alien to love, or to a love that is somehow unhealthy. Considered in the context of this group, "The Last of the Flock" seems not the anti-Godwinian defense of private property that it has often been taken to be, but something very nearly opposite. Although she faces an imminent and decidedly unpleasant death, the Indian woman of "Complaint" acts from a love unmixed with baser emotions. In contrast to her feelings are the emotions of other characters in the poems of this group. The idealist turned cynic, whose tale is told in "Lines Left upon a Seat in a Yew-tree," is a prototype of the Solitary of *The Excursion*. The lesson of "Lines," pounded home rather too obviously by Wordsworth, is that "The man whose eye / Is ever on himself doth look on one, / The least of Nature's works . . . ."

The unnamed old shepherd in "The Last of the Flock" has also mistaken selfish pride for love. Unless Wordsworth was as blind to the irony of this poem as only his most

[11] This technique, which seems so right in the post-Freudian world, is employed more successfully in "Strange Fits of Passion." See Geoffrey H. Hartman, *Wordsworth's Poetry, 1787–1814* (New Haven and London: Yale University Press, 1964), pp. 23–25.

unsympathetic critics would believe, the shepherd's naive confession that his paternal love waxed and waned with the fortunes of his livestock is a sure indication that the poem is not an emotional glorification of private ownership, but a subtle portrayal of the destructive effects of the most exclusive of emotions, greed, on the most expansive, love.[12] The irony may, in fact, be even deeper. Read with a complete unawareness of ironic implication, the old man's tender concern for his flock can evoke the figure of Christ the Good Shepherd. But the world of this poem is decidedly less Biblical than modern, the world of trade which converts natural objects, animals or land, into negotiable commodities. The sheep of the Christian parables are symbols for men. The sheep of this poem are symbols only in economics: the shepherd refers to his "store" and his "stock," and mourns their loss as "the end of all my gains." Consider this account of the benefits of private property:

> "To wicked deeds I was inclined,
> And wicked fancies crossed my mind;
> And every man I chanced to see,
> I thought he knew some ill of me:
> No peace, no comfort could I find,
> No ease, within doors or without."   (ll. 71–76)

[12] See esp. the following lines from stanza IX:
> "Sir! 'twas a precious flock to me,
> As dear as my own children be;
> For daily with my growing store
> I loved my children more and more.
> Alas! it was an evil time;
> God cursed me in my sore distress;
> I prayed, yet every day I thought
> I loved my children less; . . ."   (ll. 81–88)

Loss ennobles the Indian woman; it reduces the shepherd to primitive cupidity. She translates death into the loss of a loved one; he experiences spiritual death in the loss of possessions. Love and imagination are mutually invigorating; pride and avarice are the natural enemies of both. If "The Female Vagrant" seems to imply an attitude toward private property opposite to that of "The Last of the Flock," we might notice that the heroine of the former does not think of her paternal farm as a possession, but as a thing that possesses, a spirit of place that is decidedly more spiritual than material. However Godwin conceived of private ownership, Wordsworth seems rightly to insist that it is neither good nor evil in itself.

The principle governing the organization of the remaining five groups of poems is realized most fully in "Tintern Abbey" and *The Prelude*. Beginning with two studies of the primitive imagination manifesting itself in superstitious minds ("Goody Blake and Harry Gill" and "The Thorn"), Wordsworth then traces the growth of the mind from childhood to maturity. The responses of the little boy in "Anecdote for Fathers" are so instinctive as to be products more of sensation than of emotion. The dramatic conflict in both poems, between the child who "thinks" intuitively and the adult who reasons, was to become the major theme of the "Poems of the Fancy" in the edition of 1815, the self-imposed alienation of man from Nature and from children, whose actions and thoughts are natural.[13] Like pride, also the creation of adults, maturity itself is, or threatens to be, a force for division and exclusion. For this reason, Wordsworth's concept of imagination is militantly anti-rationalistic. The exclusively adult faculty, the understanding, was,

[13] This theme is discussed on pp. 84–97.

according to Wordsworth, "that false secondary power / By which we multiply distinctions."[14] The adult lives in a world of both metaphysical and moral dualisms, and his bent is toward division and separation.

The obtuse inquisitor in "Anecdote for Fathers" insists upon a fissure in both time and place, impelled by his obsession to contrast, to see that which is in terms of that which is not. His rational dualism demands a choice between Klive and Liswyn farm, between the present and the past, as if the two pairs were representatives of moral opposites. The clue to his malady is his vocabulary ("which like you *more*"? where "had you *rather* be"?),[15] and his compulsive demands are punctuated by Wordsworth with an incremental refrain ("I . . . took him by the arm," "I . . . held him by the arm," ". . . still I held him by the arm"). An apt description of the speaker's reaction to the child's innocence of dualism belongs to a later poem, the "Intimations Ode": "High instincts before which our mortal Nature / Did tremble like a guilty Thing surprised." Before the confrontation ends, the adult infection has spread: "At this my

---

[14] *Prelude*, II, 216–217. For all his insistence on the value of the mature rational powers, both in *The Prelude* and in his descriptions of poetic composition in the 1800 Preface, Wordsworth seems never quite to have trusted them. Only a reason that is really imagination by another name ("Reason in her most exalted mood," *Prelude*, XIV, 192) was satisfying to him, and it may be doubted that the "years that bring the philosophic mind" answer to his conception of imagination as reason. Wordsworth's extreme distrust of the rational is the fundamental difference between his theory of imagination and Coleridge's, and the source of Coleridge's strictures, in the *Biographia Literaria* and elsewhere, against Wordsworth's attributing to primitive societies and to infants and children the greatest imaginative power. See esp. *BL*, II, 29–49, 103–114.

[15] Italics mine.

boy hung down his head, / He blushed with shame . . . ." [16]
As in the Book of Genesis, *Paradise Lost*, and the poems of
Blake, the loss of innocence is accompanied by the tortures
of an undefined sense of guilt. The ludicrously pedantic
speaker in "We Are Seven" is also possessed. His mathe-
matical approach to a spiritual dilemma is symptomatically
incongruous. For the child, a family is an indivisible and
permanent spiritual unit. For the adult, it is a number of
objects from which units can be subtracted. For the girl,
heaven and earth are not widely separated physical locations,
nor are life and death mutually exclusive states of being.
Her brother and sister no longer run and play with her, but
her continued association with them is both intimate and
natural.

The stage of maturity tends toward exclusion and
division, but there are moments and there are means of
recovery. The most reliable and potent of these means is
love. Love in its various forms is the theme of the remaining
groups, and this theme is developed as well in the poems
first printed in this edition, those of volume two. In
familiar Wordsworthian language, this theme can be called
"Love of Nature Leading to Love of Man," and the first
poem of the fifth group, "It is the first mild day of March,"
states it explicitly:

> Love, now a universal birth,
> From heart to heart is stealing,
> From earth to man, from man to earth:
> —It is the hour of feeling.   (ll. 21–24)

[16] The speaker's explanation of his motive for asking his son the
question is worth recalling as a plausible instance of Wordsworthian
irony:

> A day it was when I could bear

The other three poems of this group focus simultaneously on two operations of love, one functioning within the poem itself and the other within the mind of the reader whose sympathetic imagination meets the prerequisite announced in "Simon Lee":

> O Reader! had you in your mind
> Such stores as silent thought can bring,
> O gentle Reader! you would find
> A tale in every thing.   (ll. 73–76)

This proviso is not the poet's excuse for having no story to tell, but the other side of Wordsworth's recommendation of "a wise passiveness." This passive receptiveness to impulses from Nature is not an end in itself but a preliminary stage, during which the growing imagination prepares itself for later exertions. In his elaborate arrangement of the poems in 1815 and in his description of the poetic process in the Preface to *Lyrical Ballads*, Wordsworth shows that he regards this relatively passive stage as a "seed-time," a time for building up in memory stores of silent thought that will provide nourishment for the mind in its leaner seasons. During this period of apparent indolence, "Even in what seem our most unfruitful hours" (*Prelude*, V, 363), the growing boy, particularly the young poet to be, participates in an inscrutable process that will make him a man of "more lively sensibility, more enthusiasm and tenderness . . . greater knowledge of human nature, and a more comprehensive soul, than are supposed

---

> Some fond regrets to entertain;
> With so much happiness to spare,
> I could not feel a pain.   (ll. 13–16)

There is no doubt that the question causes the boy pain.

to be common among mankind . . . .[17] That such was the pattern of Wordsworth's development we know from remarks in the Preface to *Lyrical Ballads*.[18] Because as the Romantics used the term *poet* it embraced both participants in the poetic experience, Wordsworth's understanding of the growth of imagination led him to expect from his readers an imagination comparable in intensity to the poet's own. Only such readers would insure that a poem could duplicate the operations of Nature on the human mind, could act as "A power like one of Nature's" (*Prelude*, XIII, 312).[19]

The poems of the fifth group deal principally with the movement of love "from heart to heart"; those of the sixth concentrate on love which moves "from earth to man," and make use of a contrast between man and natural creatures that is one of Wordsworth's favorite techniques. The contrast is introduced explicitly in the first of the group, "Lines Written in Early Spring," wherein the speaker expresses the conflict in his mind between the impulse to love that is Nature's gift and the human capacity for cruelty. Of all creatures in Nature only man is unhappy, or is, in fact, capable of unhappiness. For a faith "that every flower / Enjoys the air it breathes" the constantly disturbing

[17] Preface to *Lyrical Ballads*, *PW*, II, 393.

[18] The passage to which I refer is seldom quoted and discussed, but is an important part of the description of poetry as "the spontaneous overflow of powerful feelings." It begins, ". . . and though this be true, Poems to which any value can be attached were never produced on any variety of subjects but by a man who, being possessed of more than usual organic sensibility, had also thought long and deeply," and continues to the end of the paragraph. *PW*, II, 387–388.

[19] Undeniably, the tone of Wordsworth's criticisms of popular taste is defensive, but they are perfectly consonant with his theory of imagination as a requirement for both poet and reader.

fact is "What man has made of man." The opposition between natural feeling and intellect is of course fundamental in Wordsworth's poetry. Only man can be unhappy and only man has rational powers. Wordsworth made the obvious connection between these two assumptions, and the four poems of this group are portraits of unquiet humanity set against the peace of Nature.[20]

Of the last five poems of volume one, two, "The Idiot Boy" and "The Mad Mother" ("Her Eyes Are Wild"), are obviously related in style and theme; both concern the power of love to surmount all obstacles, whether abnormality of the lover or of the loved one. The last poems, "The Ancient Mariner" and "Tintern Abbey," are less obviously, but no less significantly related. Both are fitting summations of the major theme of the volume. These poems complement each other, demonstrating that by whatever means and in whatever circumstances the pulse of love that quickens Nature is accessible to man, whether his imagination has been nourished through the agency of superstition or through the natural but disciplined development sketched in "Tintern Abbey." In the first edition, Coleridge's poem had come first and Wordsworth's last, an arrangement easily defended as sound publishing practice. The later arrangement was more consonant with Wordsworth's growing interest in the total effect of a body of poems.

My discussion of volume one of the 1800 edition is not offered as a series of explications, even of the few poems

---

[20] On this point see esp. David Ferry, *The Limits of Mortality* (Middletown: Wesleyan University Press, 1959), *passim*. See also Robert Langbaum, "The Mysteries of Identity: A Theme in Modern Literature," *American Scholar*, XXXIV (1965), 569–586. To the image of the "beguiling sea" in "Lines Written While Sailing" cf. the "smiling sea" of "Peele Castle."

considered in some detail. It is meant rather to indicate the extent to which the desire for a unified effect from his poems came to influence Wordsworth's editorial practice, and to demonstrate that the location of a poem in his collected works is an important consideration in any full explication of it.

In May, 1807, Wordsworth wrote to Lady Beaumont that his poems gathered under the heading "Sonnets to Liberty" in the *Poems* of 1807, "while they each fix the attention upon some important sentiment separately considered, do at the same time collectively make a Poem on the subject of civil Liberty and national independence."[21] The classification named in the letter is one of five in the two volumes of 1807, but there is no discernible single principle upon which these classifications are based, and there are many poems not classified at all. Of his classifications, two indicate the occasions on which the poems were composed and two indicate genres. On the whole there is less evidence of consistent design in the arrangement of the poems than is shown in the 1800 edition of *Lyrical Ballads*. The most important classification in the *Poems* of 1807 is "Moods of my own Mind," because in its emphasis on the mind of the poet it suggests the degree to which Wordsworth's continuing investigation of "the powers requisite for the production of poetry" was beginning to influence his organization of poems.[22] In fact, six of the thirteen poems in this group were included under the heading "Poems of the Imagination" in the edition of 1815.

Except for the Preface of 1815, Wordsworth's only

[21] *The Letters of William and Dorothy Wordsworth: The Middle Years*, ed. Ernest de Selincourt (Oxford: Oxford University Press, 1937), I, 127; hereafter cited as *MY*.
[22] Preface of 1815, *PW*, II, 431.

known detailed explanation of his principles of organization is contained in a letter to Coleridge written in May, 1809. Given his uncertainty at this time concerning the precise arrangement he wanted to follow and given also his notoriously rambling epistolary style, it is impossible to derive from this letter a completely accurate representation of the arrangement that he proposed for his poems when he first brought them together for a collected edition—especially since this arrangement seems to have kept changing as he was writing the letter. In fact, he seems to have been thinking out loud, and the pen, never for him a comfortable instrument, was too slow for his thoughts. The table printed below reproduces, as accurately as seems possible, the plan of arrangement and classification described in 1809:[23]

I. Poems Relating to Childhood
   1. "Foresight"
   2. "The Pet Lamb"
   3. "Alice Fell"
   4. "Lucy Gray"
   5. "We Are Seven"
   6. "Anecdote for Fathers"
   7. "Rural Architecture"
   8. "The Idle Shepherd Boys"
   9. "To H.C." [Hartley Coleridge]
   10. "There Was a Boy"
   11. "Ode: Intimations of Immortality . . ."

[23] For convenience, I have sometimes changed Wordsworth's titles to those of the one-volume Oxford Wordsworth (Oxford Standard Authors Series). In the letter some poems are tentatively assigned to one group and then, some sentences later, to another. Further explanations of inconsistencies in the letter will appear in subsequent notes. The letter appears in *MY*, I, 307–309.

II. Affections of Youth and Early Maturity
    1. "The Sparrow's Nest"[24]
    2. "The Redbreast Chasing the Butterfly"
    3. "To a Butterfly" ["I've watched you now"]
    4. "To a Butterfly" ["Stay near me"][25]
    5. "Strange fits of passion"
    6. "She dwelt among the untrodden ways"
    7. "I travelled among unknown men"
    8. "Three years she grew"
    9. "A slumber did my spirit seal"[26]
    10. "She was a Phantom of delight"
    11. "Louisa"
    12. "To a Young Lady" ["Dear Child of Nature"]
    13. "A Complaint"
    14. "'Tis said that some have died for love"
    15. "Ellen Irwin"
    16. "Ruth"[27]

III. Poems Relating to Natural Objects and their Influence on the Mind[28]
    1. "To the Daisy" ["Bright Flower!"]

[24] Wordsworth first considers placing this poem and "the Butterfly" (Butterflies?) in the first group.

[25] The inclusion of poems nrs. 2–4 is a reasonable conjecture. Wordsworth refers simply to "the Butterflies," giving neither titles nor number.

[26] To avoid the old argument over which lyrics really should be called "Lucy poems," I have included all popular candidates for this title. The name "Lucy" appears in all but one of the poems, and that one, "A Slumber Did My Spirit Seal" is the companion to "Three Years She Grew." Wordsworth's only reference is "those about Lucy."

[27] Wordsworth considers concluding this group either with "Ruth" or "The Brothers," but seems to feel that "this last might be placed elsewhere."

[28] Wordsworth remarks that the poems of this group are named "at Random," but in fact most of the poems named first were later to be

2. "To the Daisy" ["In youth from rock to rock"]
3. "To the Same Flower"
4. "To the Daisy" ["Sweet Flower!"]
5. "The Small Celandine"
6. "To the Small Celandine"
7. "To the Same Flower"
8. "I wandered lonely as a cloud"[29]
9. "O Nightingale! thou surely art"
10. "The Green Linnet"
11. "The Waterfall and the Eglantine"
12. "The Oak and the Broom"
13. "Written with a Slate Pencil..." ["Stranger! this Willock of mis-shapen stones"]
14. "Written with a Pencil..." ["Rude is this Edifice"][30]
15. "Lines Written in Early Spring"
16. "A Whirl-Blast from behind the Hill"
17. "The Kitten and Falling Leaves"[31]
18. "To the Cuckoo"
19. "The sun has long been set"[32]
20. "Nutting"
21. "Tintern Abbey"[33]

---

called "Poems of the Fancy" and three of the later ones, "Poems of the Imagination." This group, he says, "would be numerous."

[29] Again, my conjectures. Wordsworth mentions only "the daisies," "the Celandines," "the daffodils."

[30] Wordsworth writes "Poem on Rydale Island" and "on Grasmere."

[31] "Fidelity" and poems "concerning Tom Hutchinson's dog" are mentioned after "The Kitten," but Wordsworth then remarks that they might better be placed elsewhere.

[32] Wordsworth writes, "the Cuckoo Poems."

[33] Near the end of the letter, Wordsworth states that "The Blind Highland Boy" should be placed in the third class, but does not say where.

IV. Poems on the Naming of Places[34]

V. Poems Relating to Human Life

First Group: Poems Appealing to the Understanding through the Imagination
1. "The Reverie of Poor Susan"
2. "Beggars"
3. "Simon Lee"
4. "The Last of the Flock"
5. "Goody Blake and Harry Gill"
6. "The Thorn"
7. "To a Highland Girl"
8. "Resolution and Independence"
9. "Hart-Leap Well"

Second Group: Poems Appealing to the Imagination through the Understanding
1. The political sonnets (unspecified)
2. "Character of the Happy Warrior"
3. "Rob Roy's Grave"
4. "Personal Talk"
5. "A Poet's Epitaph"
6. "Ode to Duty"
7. "To the Sons of Burns"

Third Group: Poems Relating to the Maternal Feeling, Connubial or Parental
1. "The Sailor's Mother"
2. "The Emigrant Mother"
3. "The Affliction of Margaret—"
4. "Her Eyes Are Wild"
5. "The Idiot Boy"

[34] The poems in this class are not named, presumably because this classification had already appeared in the second edition of *Lyrical Ballads*.

VI. Poems on Old Age
    1. "Animal Tranquillity and Decay"
    2. "Though narrow be that old Man's cares"
    3. "The Childless Father"
    4. "The Two Thieves"
    5. "The Matron of Jedborough"
    6. "Matthew"
    7. "The Two April Mornings"
    8. "The Fountain"[35]
    9. "The Old Cumberland Beggar"
   10. "Michael"[36]

According to the letter, poems were to be arranged on two complementary principles: the classes were to be composed of poems relating to the various stages of man's life, and the poems within each class were to be so ordered as to "ascend in a gradual scale of imagination."[37] At this time there was apparently no plan to classify the poems according to the faculties of mind most active in producing them. Instead the sole basis of organization was to be a schematic presentation of the growth of the human mind from childhood through old age, with each stage of this process represented by at least one group of poems. The article of faith that gave meaning to this arrangement is summed up in the lines from "My Heart Leaps Up" that Wordsworth chose as a motto for the first group of poems, and later prefixed to the "Intimations Ode:" "The Child is father of the Man; / And I could wish my days to be / Bound each to each by natural

[35] Wordsworth writes, "those relating to Matthew."
[36] Wordsworth was uncertain, but thought perhaps that this poem should be the last in this class and should also "conclude the whole."
[37] This quotation and all others in my discussion of this arrangement not attributed to another source are from the letter of 1809, *MY*, I, 307–309.

piety." Human identity is single, hence, so Wordsworth believed, as permanent as the forms of Nature. Both are earthly reflections of divine permanence, valued "chiefly as an 'imperfect shadowing forth' of what [man] is incapable of seeing."[38] His first explicit statement of this faith appears in the Preface to *Lyrical Ballads*, wherein he speaks of his "deep impression of certain inherent and indestructible qualities of the human mind, and likewise of certain powers in the great and permanent objects that act upon it, which are equally inherent and indestructible."[39]

In 1809 Wordsworth's idea of the total effect of his poems and of the place of each poem and each group of poems was determined by his faith in the unity and continuity of human identity. For this reason he tried to avoid any implication that his classes represent isolated moments in the growth of the mind, by being careful to show how each stage of growth evolves from the previous one and shades into the next—as imperceptibly and as meaningfully as do landscape and observer in "Tintern Abbey." As with the mind itself, so with Wordsworth's arrangement of poems. Each would ascend gradually on a scale of imagination so that the gap between its youthful and mature manifestations would be narrowed, might, in fact, not be felt at all by one who reads the poems in the order prescribed by Wordsworth.

Throughout this arrangement there is evidence of his attempt to devise a way of considering his past that could

[38] "Essay, Supplementary to the Preface" (first published in 1815), *PW*, II, 412.

[39] *PW*, II, 389. Whether or not Wordsworth believed in theories of pre-existence, he implies in the "Intimations Ode" that certain qualities in the human mind are indestructible *because* they are inherent, that is, innate.

somehow recognize the passage of time and changes in personality without fragmenting the ages of man into separable units. Long before 1809 he had adopted such a perspective and described its delicate balance in the following lines from *The Prelude*:

> A tranquillising spirit presses now
> On my corporeal frame, so wide appears
> The vacancy between me and those days [of childhood]
> Which yet have such self-presence in my mind,
> That, musing on them, often do I seem
> Two consciousnesses, conscious of myself
> And of some other Being.   (II, 27–33)

A vacancy which is not a vacancy after all, but a self-presence in the mind, and a sense of two beings that nevertheless is affirmed by one imagination. These lines express succinctly, though with characteristically Wordsworthian paradox, his conception of the mind, which firmly locates time, as Kant had done, in the mind of man—his servant not his master.

True to this belief, Wordsworth emphasized in the poems relating to childhood not the child's reactions, as some critics still believe, but "such feelings as rise in the mind in after life in direct contemplation of . . . [childhood]." Their primary subject is not the mind and experience of children, but that mind and that experience reflected upon by an adult who knows that the child is father of man and, because he knows, can bring to past experiences a vision that fuses past and present. Thus, for example, in "There Was a Boy," the often-denounced final stanza, which depicts the speaker of the poem standing mute over the grave of the Winander boy, is not meant to commemorate the boy's untimely death. It is rather the speaker's experience that evokes the memorial; or, to paraphrase a familiar passage from the Preface to *Lyrical Ballads*, it is the feeling rising in the mind of the speaker that gives importance to the action and situation of the boy, and not the action and situation to the feeling.[40]

For purposes of the present study, the most important of the groups mentioned in the letter is the one composed of poems "relating to natural objects and their influence on the mind, either as growing or in an advanced state." It seems likely from this description that Wordsworth planned to divide this group into two parts, the first composed of poems relating to the influence of Nature on a growing mind, the second, of its influence on a mature mind. In preparing his first collected edition, he did in fact divide this class, but in such a way as to emphasize not stages in mental growth but differences between poetic faculties. Of the (probably) twenty-one poems of this class all but five were classified in 1815 as either "Poems of the Fancy" or "Poems of the Imagination."

A division was also planned for the group of poems "relating to human life," but in this case the distinction was based on the reader's mental faculties rather than the poet's. One group would consist of poems "interesting to a

[40] *PW*, II, 388–389. For a particularly vigorous criticism of the last stanza see F. W. Bateson, *Wordsworth: A Re-Interpretation* (2nd ed.; London: Longmans, Green and Co., 1963), pp. 21–27. Stephen M. Parrish has applied Wordsworth's dramatic principles to a number of poems from *Lyrical Ballads*. See "Dramatic Technique in the *Lyrical Ballads*," *PMLA*, LXXIV (1959), 85–97; "'The Thorn': Wordsworth's Dramatic Monologue," *ELH*, XXIV (1957), 153–163; "The Wordsworth-Coleridge Controversy," *PMLA*, LXXIII (1958), 367–374; "Wordsworth and Coleridge on Meter," *Journal of English and Germanic Philology*, LIX (1960), 41–49.

meditative or imaginative mind, either from the moral
importance of the pictures or from the employment they
give to the understanding, affected through the imagination,
and to the higher faculties."[41] The second would include
poems "relating to the social and civic duties, and chiefly
interesting to the imagination through the understanding,
and not to the understanding through the imagination."
The weight of meaning in these descriptions is carried by
the alternate prepositions *to* and *through*; the distinction is
determined by whether the understanding or the imagination
initiates a given experience. Experiences presented through
poetry appeal to both faculties, but they appeal directly
only to one *or* the other. As poems appealing directly to the
imagination Wordsworth named "Beggars," "The Thorn,"
"To a Highland Girl," and "Resolution and Independence"
—all later included under "Poems of the Imagination"—
and as poems appealing first to the understanding, "Character of the Happy Warrior," "Ode to Duty," and the
political sonnets. The major differences in style and subject
matter between these groups resulted from Wordsworth's
choosing to appeal directly either to the rational or to the

[41] Cf. Karl Kroeber's remark that "the Romantic visionary lyric is
a further step toward the conscious addressing of lyric poetry immediately to the imagination rather than to the imagination through
the discursive intelligence," in *Romantic Narrative Art* (Madison:
University of Wisconsin Press, 1960), p. 62. Presumably Wordsworth
meant by "understanding" in this context what it usually meant to
both him and Coleridge, the narrow, purely rational faculty which is
inferior to both reason and imagination. Their distinction between
understanding and reason was probably derived, as most scholars
believe, from Kant's *Verstand* and *Vernunft*. Both Wordsworth and
Coleridge appear to equate the understanding with the term *reason* as
it was generally used in the eighteenth century, especially by writers
of the French Enlightenment.

imaginative faculties of his readers. That decision made, he adopted the mode of expression most likely to make that appeal effectively.

Sometime between 1809 and 1815 Wordsworth made a major alteration in his plan of organization.[42] The Preface to the edition of 1815 begins with two lists, first of "the powers requisite for the production of poetry," and next of various kinds of poems. In the first list are observation and description, sensibility, reflection, imagination and fancy, invention, and judgment; in the second are the narrative, the dramatic, the lyrical, the idyllium, the didactic, and the satiric.[43] These two lists account for two of the three essential ingredients in the making of poems. Wordsworth calls the third "the materials of Poetry," and explains that these materials are either collected or created by one or more of the mental faculties named in the first list and then "are cast, by means of various moulds, into divers forms," named in his second list.[44]

Wordsworth adopted principles of classification that correspond to these three ingredients of poems: "It is deducible from the above, that poems, apparently miscellaneous, may with propriety be arranged either with

[42] But cf. Beatty, *William Wordsworth*, p. 199: ". . . the elaborate classification of his poems [in the edition of 1815] was . . . little more than the enlargement of a plan roughly sketched out ten years before." Although Beatty speaks of "ten years before" 1815, he was referring to the letter of 1809.

[43] *PW*, II, 431–433. The idyllium is described as being "descriptive chiefly either of the processes and appearances of external nature, as the Seasons of Thomson; or of characters, manners, and sentiments, as are Shenstone's School-mistress, The Cotter's Saturday Night of Burns, The Twa Dogs of the same Author." Wordsworth would include in this category all "loco-descriptive poetry."

[44] *PW*, II, 432.

reference to the powers of mind *predominant* in the production of them; or to the mould in which they are cast; or, lastly, to the subjects to which they relate."[45] Using these three methods of classification, Wordsworth went on to create that mixture of categories which damned his organization of poems to neglect or faint praise.

The confusion lurking in his apparently simple procedure seems to have occurred to Wordsworth in the very act of composing his explanation of it. In any event, his confident tone soon dissipates as he proceeds to anticipate and unwittingly to encourage the most frequently expressed objections to his classifications: "Where there is more imagination than fancy in a poem, it is placed under the head of imagination, and *vice versa*. Both the above classes might without impropriety have been enlarged from that consisting of 'Poems founded on the Affections'; as might this latter from those, and from the class 'proceeding from Sentiment and Reflection.'"[46] The confusion is all but complete, and even the most determined reader of the Preface must have wondered whether any clear idea could be concealed under so much ambiguity.

De Selincourt was right to call this scheme a compromise. By 1815, and long before, compromise had become a habit of Wordsworth's mind. The formality and the catholicity of his new Preface are testimony to this habit, as are his attempts to mediate between two poetic and philosophic traditions by producing poems in such a range of styles as to invite readers of the most diverse tastes. The plan of organization contemplated in 1809 was not simple or totally self-consistent, but it was in both respects superior

[45] *PW*, II, 433.
[46] *PW*, II, 434.

to that which he attempted to describe and which he incorporated in the edition of 1815. It was also more daring, since it ignored traditional principles of categorizing poems and emphasized almost exclusively the growth of a poet's mind. During the years that separated these two plans, Wordsworth may have pondered glumly the scorn heaped by reviewers of the *Poems* of 1807 upon his classification of some poems as "Moods of my own Mind," who cited this title as evidence of a boorish egocentrism. Whatever the reasons, in the edition of 1815 he appears to have abandoned the cardinal motive of the earlier plan, substituting for an emphasis on arrangement an emphasis on classification. The plan of 1809 made no provision for a grouping of poems according to the faculties most active in their production, or according to genre and subject matter, the only three bases of classification identified in 1815 as appropriate principles of organization.

The guiding principle of the earlier plan is not forgotten in the Preface of 1815, but it is disguised as a mere statement of practice, and mentioned almost as if it were an afterthought: ". . . that the work may more obviously correspond with the course of human life, and for the sake of exhibiting in it the three requisites of a legitimate whole, a beginning, a middle, and an end, [the poems] have been also arranged, *as far as it was possible*, according to an order of time, commencing with Childhood, and terminating with Old Age, Death, and Immortality."[47] And even here Wordsworth cloaks the revolutionary implications of this procedure with an appeal to the venerable conception of "a legitimate whole."

This attempt to accommodate diverse principles with

[47] *PW*, II, 433. Italics mine.

diverse implications was no more successful than such attempts usually are. Whether intentionally or not, Wordsworth permitted classification to usurp upon arrangement and thus gained for his bold portrait of the mind of man the indifference that greets daring creeds whose daring is obscured. The system of organization adopted in 1815 was not merely a compromise, but a retreat. It is, nevertheless, Wordsworth's system, and imperfect though it is, it deserves more attention that it has been given.

4

The Edition of 1815: Classification

Not so many years ago, Arthur Beatty remarked that Wordsworth was "judged in his entirety by the *Preface* of 1815" and that the Preface to *Lyrical Ballads* was hardly known at all.[1] This was an accurate assessment of the status of these essays in 1921. Today, thanks in part to Beatty's own exposition of the earlier preface, the roles of the two are reversed. The first is widely and well known; the Preface of 1815 is read only by a very few, almost never included in selections of Wordsworth's verse, and censured by those few who do write about it.[2] The general unpopularity of this preface has a great deal to do with its date of composition, with, that is, the liberal reaction against the later works and character of Wordsworth that has crept into Wordsworthian criticism since the days of Byron and Shelley. The New Critics of our century have not been exceptionally kind to Wordsworth, but they have helped his reputation indirectly by making unfashionable such

[1] Arthur Beatty, *William Wordsworth: His Doctrine and Art in their Historical Relations* (3rd ed.; Madison: University of Wisconsin Press, 1960), pp. 14–15.

[2] Herbert Read's description of the Preface as "the pedantic afterthoughts of a poet already jealous of his own past" is harsh but not atypical. *Wordsworth* (London: Jonathan Cape, 1930), p. 161.

extra-literary perspectives as those that so frequently colored the judgments of critics even in this century.[3] Despite the more rigorously aesthetic principles of modern critics, however, a lingering image of the lost leader, the Anglican Tory of Rydal Mount continues to insure the popularity of the earlier preface and the obscurity of the later.

Wordsworth himself seems to have regarded the first preface as an "occasional" piece, written solely to prepare his readers for boldly experimental poems, and in 1815 no longer either very appropriate or relevant. For this reason he moved the earlier preface to the end of the second volume of the two-volume edition of 1815, and in each edition thereafter it appeared in the last volume. As an introduction to the Preface of 1815, Wordsworth wrote the following description of the earlier one: "The observations prefixed to that portion of these Volumes, which was published many years ago, under the title of 'Lyrical Ballads,' have so little of a special application to the greater part, perhaps, of this collection, as subsequently enlarged and diversified, that they could not with any propriety stand as an Introduction to it."[4] By implication, then, the new preface was designed to enunciate Wordsworth's mature view of poetry in general, rather than to expound a theory limited to a special kind of poem.

An indication of this new purpose is the very formal method of this preface. It opens with the two broadly ambitious enumerations discussed in my last chapter and is

[3] James V. Logan gives a useful summary of the genesis and career of Wordsworth as "apostate" in *Wordsworthian Criticism* (Columbus: Ohio State University Press, 1947), pp. 83–99.

[4] *PW*, II, 431.

permeated with Wordsworth's desire to devise a comprehensive, rational, and objective account of poetry as craft. He does not speak at length here, as he had in the first preface, of the exalted mission of the poet. His voice is no longer the prophet's, but the gentleman poet's. He writes not a Romantic "Defence of Poetry," but a formal treatise on the artful (and artificial) manipulation of words. These are the facts behind the often repeated observation that the Preface of 1815 appears to be less the work of a Romantic than of a Neo-classical writer.[5]

This characteristic of the Preface is not in itself cause for reproof in our day of amicability and mutual respect between scholars of the eighteenth and nineteenth centuries. It is, on the other hand, cause for confusion among students of Wordsworth, particularly those who wish to muster sympathy for his way of organizing poems. All of this confusion accurately reflects Wordsworth's indecision and uncertainty. In the Preface of 1815 he emphasizes the classification of poems; in the poems themselves it is arrangement that most nearly succeeds in achieving the goal he set for himself. The classification of poems according to the faculties most active in their creation or according to genre or occasion has not proved to be, and I think cannot be proved to be, "a commentary unostentatiously directing the reader's attention" toward some unified impression and effect. By subordinating the order of his poems to the

---

[5] See, e.g., Meyer H. Abrams, *The Mirror and the Lamp* (New York: W. W. Norton and Company, 1958), pp. 181–182; H. W. Garrod, *Wordsworth: Lectures and Essays* (Oxford: Oxford University Press, 1923), p. 162; John Jones, *The Egotistical Sublime* (London: Chatto and Windus, 1954), p. 45; Herbert A. Lindenberger, *On Wordsworth's "Prelude"* (Princeton: Princeton University Press, 1963), pp. 38–39.

demands of conflicting principles of organization, Wordsworth bequeathed to future readers a doubt of his methods that soon turned into neglect of them. For with the exception of Dowden scholars have focused their attention on the classifications of poems in the collected editions, ignoring almost completely the more useful feature of Wordsworth's system of organization. It is ironic that Wordsworth should have exhibited the greatest concern to explain the distinctive characteristics of poetic faculties at a time when his own imaginative powers had notably diminished.

Few subjects in Wordsworthian criticism have received more consideration than the distinction between fancy and imagination, and few have produced more acrimony or less agreement. Some critics have insisted that no useful distinction exists, others that the only useful distinction is not Wordsworth's but Coleridge's.[6] Even the few who have taken Wordsworth's distinction seriously and defended it have not reached agreement over precisely what it is. Much of this confusion was inevitable, a natural consequence

[6] Garrod considered the distinction "famous, but useless" (*Wordsworth*, p. 145n) and Read called the two faculties "the twin humbugs of romantic criticism" (*Wordsworth*, p. 162); W. K. Wimsatt, Jr. and Cleanth Brooks, believing that "Coleridge did not differ vitally from Wordsworth about 'imagination,'" very quickly concentrate on the former "as the more articulate and more theoretical spokesman of the two." The consummate irony of these learned and gifted critics constantly threatens to nudge aside their sympathy with the subject of their discussion, but despite this their chapter on "Imagination: Wordsworth and Coleridge" contains excellent analyses of Romantic theory. Their conclusion, however, that the distinction between imagination and fancy "was intended as a division between bad and good form in poetry" greatly diminishes both the distinction and their discussion of it. *Literary Criticism: A Short History* (New York: Alfred A. Knopf, 1957), pp. 388–389, 404.

of Wordsworth's own. Because, as R. D. Havens observed, Wordsworth usually thought of the activity of imagination as "the transformation wrought within the mind rather than any expression of such a transformation in a work of art," he understandably found it difficult to explain objectively an impression decidedly subjective, an event occurring in his own mind.[7]

One apparent result of this difficulty is that Wordsworth made not one but two distinctions between fancy and imagination, one in his prose and another in *The Prelude*. The presence of two distinctions has seldom been acknowledged. Arthur Beatty, for example, concluded from his study of *The Prelude* as a poetic illustration of David Hartley's associationist psychology, that fancy and imagination are not so much separate faculties as stages "of the mind in its growth," imagination "appearing first as Fancy in Youth." As evidence for his belief that Wordsworth "clearly regarded Fancy as being transformed into Imagination," he cited the following passage from the Preface of 1815: ". . . 'An address to an Infant,' which the Reader will find under the Class of Fancy in the present Volumes, exhibits something of this communion and interchange of instruments and functions between the two powers; and is, accordingly, placed last in the class, as a preparation for that of Imagination which follows." As further documentation Beatty pointed to the following lines from *The Prelude*:

> Yes, having track'd the main essential Power,
> Imagination, up her way sublime,
> In turn might Fancy also be pursued

[7] R. D. Havens, *The Mind of a Poet* (Baltimore: Johns Hopkins Press, 1941), p. 220.

Through all her transmigrations, till she too
Was purified, had learn'd to ply her craft
By judgment steadied.   (1805, XIII, 289–294)[8]

Actually, neither passage supports Beatty's interpretation. The phrase "communion and interchange" does not imply that fancy is an early stage of imagination, but that the two powers operate simultaneously. And the lines from *The Prelude* speak of a fancy that, like imagination, passes through stages until, also like imagination, it is steadied by judgment and so becomes a mature faculty. Hence, it is misleading to identify fancy as exclusively a power of youth. Realizing this, we should not share Crabb Robinson's surprise that Wordsworth could "speak of his poems of fancy as if he deemed them not inferior to his poems of imagination."[9]

There is impressive support, nevertheless, for Beatty's interpretation. In Book VIII of *The Prelude*, one can find the youthful imagination described in terms that Wordsworth used of fancy in the Preface of 1815. More important, in stating his intention to arrange his poems so as to exhibit "an order of time" from childhood to maturity, he invited the inference that his placing the poems of fancy before those of imagination indicates that fancy is the faculty of youth and imagination of maturity.[10] Because of Words-

[8] Beatty, *William Wordsworth*, pp. 168, 204, 191. Beatty's quotation from the Preface is in *PW*, II, 442.

[9] *Henry Crabb Robinson on Books and their Writers*, ed. Edith J. Morley (London: J. M. Dent and Sons Ltd., 1938), I, 96.

[10] For a fuller statement of this interpretation, see Beatty, *William Wordsworth*, esp. chaps. V–IX. Beatty thought of fancy as a natural activity in youth but as a threat to imagination in maturity. I agree that an increasing reliance on the mode of fancy was either a cause or a result of Wordsworth's decline, but, whether rationalizing or not, Wordsworth insisted that fancy, though not so grand as imagination, had important functions.

worth's two formulations of the distinction between them, any search for a consistent theory of the powers of fancy and imagination must rely most on his final published statement on the subject, the Preface of 1815, and on the poems attributed to these faculties appearing in his collected editions. Accordingly, the discussion that follows is meant to provide a context for the classifications "Poems of the Fancy" and "Poems of the Imagination" as first publicly explained and adopted in the edition of 1815.

There is no hint of a distinction between fancy and imagination in the Preface to *Lyrical Ballads*. The two terms appear together in only one sentence, and they might reasonably be considered simply an instance of Wordsworth's affection for reduplication: ". . . [the poet] will feel that there is no necessity to trick out or to elevate nature: and the more industriously he applies this principle, the deeper will be his faith that no words which *his* fancy or imagination can suggest will be to be compared with those which are the emanations of reality and truth."[11] In the second edition of *Lyrical Ballads*, in which the Preface first appeared, there also appeared for the first time an explanatory note to "The Thorn," in which Wordsworth attempted, unsuccessfully, to disarm critics of his loquacious narrator by distinguishing between two kinds of minds: "Superstitious men are almost always men of slow faculties and deep feelings; their minds are not loose, but adhesive; they have a reasonable share of imagination, by which word I mean the faculty which produces impressive effects out of simple elements; but they are utterly destitute of fancy, the power by which pleasure and surprise are excited by sudden varieties of situation and an accumulated imagery."[12]

[11] *PW*, II, 394.
[12] *PW*, II, 512.

Because Wordsworth did not reprint this note in editions after 1805, it has seldom been examined by critics, who evidently assumed that Wordsworth considered his explanation of fancy and imagination in 1815 to have rendered the earlier formulation unnecessary. Wordsworth probably thought so too, but in fact it is a very helpful complement to the more elaborate later explanation, and it is in many ways clearer.

The most important difference between Wordsworth's two comments on fancy and imagination in 1800 and the discussion of them in 1815 is that the first are decidedly more modest in their claims for these powers. In the Preface to *Lyrical Ballads*, both faculties are emphatically distinguished from "reality and truth," to which their operations are professedly inferior; and in seeming to identify superstition and imagination, the note to "The Thorn" permits one to doubt that the "impressive effects" which imagination can produce are any more valid than creations of superstition. Assuredly, Wordsworth does proclaim in 1800 the doctrine that poetry can reveal truths hidden from the man of science, but in the kind of poetry he envisioned then, the role of imagination as a faculty that *creates* truths was as yet apparently not a firm belief. Or it may have been, as Geoffrey Hartman has suggested, a belief from which Wordsworth shrank in fear, until the act of composing lines on his crossing of the Alps (*Prelude*, VI, 592–616) forced him finally to acknowledge it.[13]

At least by 1804, the year he composed most of Book VI, Wordsworth was permitting himself to express forthrightly

[13] Geoffrey H. Hartman, *Wordsworth's Poetry, 1787–1814* (New Haven and London: Yale University Press, 1964), pp. 39–60, *et passim*.

a more exalted theory of imagination, and he expounds a bolder claim for this power in the Preface of 1815. In attempting to distinguish between fancy and imagination, he begins by quoting from William Taylor's *British Synonyms Discriminated*, published in 1813, what he presumably takes to be the currently accepted definitions of these terms. According to Taylor's definitions, imagination "is the faculty which *images* within the mind the phenomena of sensation," and fancy is the power to "call up, connect, or associate, at pleasure, those internal images ... so as to complete ideal representations of absent objects." Further, "the imagination is formed by patient observation; the fancy by a voluntary activity in shifting the scenery of the mind." The goal of imagination is accuracy; the goal of fancy is to produce "decorations" which are "original and striking." "Imagination is the power of depicting, and fancy of evoking and combining." Of Taylor's distinction Wordsworth asks, "Is not this as if a man should undertake to supply an account of a building, and be so intent upon what he had discovered of the foundation, as to conclude his task without once looking up at the superstructure?" The precise point of this analogy is not entirely clear. The word *foundation* may apply merely to etymologies, which in the next sentence Wordsworth explains were the basis of Taylor's definitions. The remainder of his discussion, however, suggests that the analogy of foundation and superstructure may apply as well to the relationship between the senses, the foundation of imaginative activity, and the higher functions for which the senses are merely a first stage. It is these higher functions that Wordsworth claims for the imagination "in the sense of the word as giving title to a class of the following

Poems"—"denoting operations of the mind" upon objects of the senses, "and processes of creation or of composition, governed by certain fixed laws."[14]

After offering very cryptic definitions of imagination ("that faculty of which the Poet is 'all compact'") and fancy ("as insinuating herself into the heart of objects with creative activity"), he presents a series of illustrations, first of imagination, then of fancy, from his own poetry and that of others. There is general agreement among critics that these illustrations do not perform adequately the task that Wordsworth assigned to them. Nevertheless, René Wellek's remark that they "merely cite very ordinary metaphorical transfers" is less than just, if I understand correctly the meaning of "ordinary metaphorical transfers."[15] Such a characterization might fairly be applied to the illustrations from Virgil, Shakespeare, and Milton; but when Wordsworth discusses those from his own poetry, he speaks with authority of a mode of symbolism that is far from ordinary. Indeed, in his comments on two of these illustrations, the opening lines of "To the Cuckoo" and the stone-sea beast image from "Resolution and Independence," he gives a succinct statement of what he conceived to be the effect of the poetic imagination, in the first poem on an image of sound, in the second on an image of sight.

In discussing these illustrations, Wordsworth consistently emphasizes that all the powers which he attributes to the imagination—conferring, abstracting, modifying, shaping, and creating—work toward a common goal, to free an object from all sense of limitation. Thus, by abstract-

[14] *PW*, II, 435–436.
[15] René Wellek, *A History of Modern Criticism* (New Haven: Yale University Press, 1955), II, 146.

ing from his experience of the cuckoo the bird's "wandering Voice," he confers on this object something which it only appears to the imagination to possess—the "seeming ubiquity of the voice." In so doing his imagination frees the bird from its physical limitations and "dispossesses the creature almost of a corporeal existence." As almost always in Wordsworth's poetry, the imagination starts from an actual sense experience, but uses that experience to escape the bonds of sense, "being tempted to this exertion of her power" by a real characteristic abstracted from a real object. The imagination is highly selective, focusing its energies on a suggestive fact presented by the senses that can release its creative power, so that objects of sense are "endowed by the mind with properties that do not inhere in them, upon an incitement from properties and qualities the existence of which is inherent and obvious." [16] This is the process at work in the lines that Wordsworth quotes from "Resolution and Independence":

> As a huge stone is sometimes seen to lie
> Couched on the bald top of an eminence,
> Wonder to all who do the same espy
> By what means it could thither come, and whence,
> So that it seems a thing endued with sense,
> Like a sea-beast crawled forth, which on a shelf
> Of rock or sand reposeth, there to sun himself.
>
> Such seemed this Man; not all alive or dead
> Nor all asleep, in his extreme old age.
> . . . .
> Motionless as a cloud the old Man stood,
> That heareth not the loud winds when they call,
> And moveth altogether if it move at all.   (ll. 57–65, 75–77)

[16] *PW*, II, 437–438.

Of these lines he says, "the conferring, the abstracting, and the modifying powers of the Imagination, immediately and mediately acting, are all brought into conjunction," and then goes on to describe the imaginative process involved:

> The stone is endowed with something of the power of life to approximate it to the sea-beast; and the sea-beast stripped of some of its vital qualities to assimilate it to the stone; which intermediate image is thus treated for the purpose of bringing the original image, that of the stone, to a nearer resemblance to the figure and the condition of the aged Man; who is divested of so much of the indications of life and motion as to bring him to the point where the two objects unite and coalesce in just comparison.[17]

The result of this process is an image neither of stone nor of sea-beast; nor is it simply of a man, but rather of an old man "not all alive or dead." By endowing an inanimate object with something approaching life and taking away from a creature actually living some of the qualities that we associate with life, Wordsworth blurs the distinction between the living man and the inanimate object. The imagination has so modified the image of the aged leech-gatherer that the boundary between man and Nature is metaphorically denied.

After offering his illustrations and a few comments on them, Wordsworth seems to conclude his analysis of this faculty. But in a subsequent passage on the subject, which is rarely quoted, he gives a valuable clue to his theory of imagination:

> The grand store-houses of enthusiastic and meditative Imagination, of poetical, as contra-distinguished from

[17] *PW*, II, 438.

human and dramatic Imagination, are the prophetic and lyrical parts of the Holy Scriptures, and the works of Milton; to which I cannot forbear to add those of Spenser. I select these writers in preference to those of ancient Greece and Rome, because the anthropomorphitism of the Pagan religion subjected the minds of the greatest poets in those countries too much to the bondage of definite form; from which the Hebrews were preserved by their abhorrence of idolatry. This abhorrence was almost as strong in out great epic Poet [Milton] .... However imbued the surface might be with classical literature, he was a Hebrew in soul; and all things tended in him towards the sublime.[18]

The emphasis on freedom from "the bondage of definite form," the association of imagination with the sublime, and the preference for the Hebrew over the classical "soul"— all these attitudes are of great importance in Wordsworth's theory of imagination; and the implications of these attitudes extend, as we shall see, far beyond aesthetics.

Wordsworth approaches the fancy by way of contrast to the imagination, and this negative approach proves more nearly successful. He begins the discussion with his well-known objection that Coleridge's definition of the fancy ("the aggregative and associative power") is "too general," because "to aggregate and to associate, to evoke and to combine, belong as well to the Imagination as to the Fancy." The difference, Wordsworth argues, is not in these activities, but is rather that "either the materials evoked and combined are different; or they are brought together under a different law, and for a different purpose." These differences he proceeds to discuss. The materials

[18] *PW*, II, 439–440.

worked upon by fancy need not "be susceptible of change in their constitution, from her touch; and, where they admit of modification, it is enough for her purpose if it be slight, limited, and evanescent." The imagination, on the other hand, "recoils from everything but the plastic, the pliant, and the indefinite."[19]

Probably no one would wish to declare that Wordsworth's comments on fancy and imagination, in the Preface of 1815 or elsewhere, are sufficiently clear. Nor can we say that he was always careful to differentiate between them. For example, we can turn to "Yarrow Visited" and find the faculties hopelessly confounded:

> And is this—Yarrow?—*This* the Stream
> Of which my fancy cherished,
> So faithfully, a waking dream?
>
> . . . .
>
> But thou, that didst appear so fair
> To fond imagination,
> Dost rival in the light of day
> Her delicate creation.   (ll. 1–3, 41–44)

But, accepting as we must such careless disregard of terminology, we can test Wordsworth's distinction on the poems that he classified as products of fancy or imagination and find, I believe, that the terms have real meaning after all. The distinction is not always clear of course. Among the "Poems of the Fancy" the one beginning "A Whirl-Blast from behind the hill" most seriously challenges Wordsworth's classification of it. It has, first of all, few of those features, to be discussed later on, that are common to poems of this class: it offers no direct moral lesson and its "meaning" permits no prose paraphrase. Moreover, its setting and

[19] *PW*, II, 441.

situation are quite similar to those of "There Was a Boy,"
one of the most characteristic of the poems of imagination.
In both poems a period of intense activity is followed by an
apparently preternatural calm:

> A Whirl-Blast from behind the hill
> Rushed o'er the wood with startling sound;
> Then—all at once the air was still.   (ll. 1–3)

>   with quivering peals,
> And long halloos, and screams, and echoes loud
> Redoubled and redoubled; concourse wild
> Of jocund din! And, when there came a pause
> Of silence . . . .   (ll. 13–17)

Both settings hold the promise of ineffable revelation. The
conclusion of the second poem is well known:

> Then, sometimes, in that silence, while he hung
> Listening, a gentle shock of mild surprise
> Has carried far into his heart the voice
> Of mountain-torrents; or the visible scene
> Would enter unawares into his mind
> With all its solemn imagery, its rocks,
> Its woods, and that uncertain heaven received
> Into the bosom of the steady lake.   (ll. 18–25)

Art decrees the form of its expression, but the experience
remains what it is, resisting translation into concepts that
would satisfy the rational powers of mind. What then of the
event that follows the similar physical situation described
in the poem of fancy? It too is seemingly unexplained:

> But see! where'er the hailstones drop
> The withered leaves all skip and hop;
> There's not a breeze—no breath of air—
> Yet here, and there, and every where

Along the floor, beneath the shade
By those embowering hollies made,
The leaves in myriads jump and spring,
As if with pipes and music rare
Some Robin Good-fellow were there,
And all those leaves, in festive glee,
Were dancing to the minstrelsy.   (ll. 12–22)

It is easy enough to say that this account is fanciful; the mention of Robin Good-fellow would seem to be sufficient warrant for such a judgment. But to leave it at this is to adopt the oversimplified distinction between fancy and imagination that would divide poems into groups according to their degree of "high seriousness." To avoid this error, one must find justification according to Wordsworth's own distinction between these terms.

In the Preface he has this to say about the mode of fancy:

> The law under which the processes of Fancy are carried on is as capricious as the accidents of things, and the effects are surprising, playful, ludicrous, amusing, tender, or pathetic, as the objects happen to be appositely produced or fortunately combined. . . . If she can win you over to her purpose, and impart to you her feelings, she cares not how unstable or transitory may be her influence, knowing that it will not be out of her power to resume it upon an apt occasion.[20]

This passage defines the great difference between the modes of the two kinds of poems: the activity of fancy is circumscribed, as that of imagination is not, by its powerlessness to transmute the materials with which it works. Because it lacks this power, fancy is dependent upon "the accidents of things"; it must, therefore, assume an essentially passive

[20] *Ibid.*

state toward Nature, waiting, so to speak, for the fortuitous circumstance. Even more to the point is another passage from this preface: "... the resemblance ... [perceived by imagination depends] less upon outline of form and feature, than upon expression and effect; less upon casual and outstanding, than upon inherent and internal properties."[21] The speaker of "A Whirl-Blast" makes only the most tenuous and arbitrary connections between object and mind. He is content to concentrate his focus on the mildly suggestive associations of a mind indulging itself, and the concluding lines seem nothing less than a desire, though hardly serious of course, to distance object from psychic event by reducing their communion to the safely familiar terms of simile:

> The leaves in myriads jump and spring,
> As if with pipes and music rare
> Some Robin Good-fellow were there,
> And all those leaves, in festive glee,
> Were dancing to the minstrelsy.

The recourse to "Robin Good-fellow" is not in itself a certain indication of fancy, but as a means of shrugging off the suggestion of visionary encounter between object and mind, it shows the experience described to be limited in duration and in implication. For, as we shall see, fancy leaves the mind at rest, imagination stimulates it to admit no rest, no limits. Most important, "A Whirl-Blast" does not "re-act upon the mind which hath performed the process [of imagination] like a new existence."[22] If my comparison of the two poems seems to imply that the poem

---

[21] *Ibid.*
[22] *PW*, II, 438.

of fancy fails to act as a poem of imagination, it has misled. A preference for the second mode of expression over the first is inevitable on more than aesthetic grounds, but Wordsworth had room for both kinds and each was given an important part in the effect he hoped to achieve by the arrangement of his poems.

5

The Edition of 1815: Arrangement

Wordsworth hoped that his special arrangement of poems would "serve as a commentary unostentatiously directing" his readers. In fact, as we know, it has usually had precisely the opposite effect, sending many readers to editions arranged according to more conventional principles. The poet himself seems to have felt never a doubt that his efforts were warranted, but he does betray some uncertainty about method and about the proper classification and position of individual poems. In 1798 and 1800 he was most concerned with the order in which the poems appeared; in 1807 he showed more interest in classification than in arrangement; and in 1809 he reversed his emphasis once more. The organizing principles that he finally settled upon are those announced in the Preface of 1815 and applied to the poems of that edition. Thereafter the organization was not substantially altered; new poems were scrupulously integrated into the pattern and a few were shifted from one class to another. Whatever its shortcomings, Wordsworth counted on this plan to produce the greatest possible total effect from poems apparently miscellaneous.

Up to this point, my inquiry into the reasons for the plan's failure has emphasized Wordsworth's own inadequate explanation of it. A second and more important reason, which will be considered here, is one for which Wordsworth cannot be held accountable: the most important feature of his organization of poems, his distinction between fancy and imagination, has not been fairly judged because the chief evidence in its favor has never been thoroughly examined. Wordsworth's comments in the Preface of 1815 were meant to be tested by application to all the "Poems of the Fancy" and "Poems of the Imagination," the two classes derived from his distinction between the powers. But unfortunately the brief illustrations in the Preface (rightly deemed inadequate and almost useless) have captured scholars' attention to such an extent that the fuller illustrations, the poems themselves, have been neglected in examinations of Wordsworth's theory of the imagination. Of the three main areas of difference which he identifies to distinguish between fancy and imagination—materials, modes of operation, and purposes—only the second figures importantly in the prefatory illustrations, whereas all three are illustrated by the poems designated according to the predominance of fancy or imagination. If we bring together prose comments and poems, we move very close to the heart of Wordsworth's poetics and philosophy.

In preparation for an analysis of the arrangement, we might well adjust our expectations in conformity with Dowden's metaphor, so that failing to find "a cast-iron series of links," we can look patiently for "a wreath of flowers lightly entwined with one another." Sometimes these wreaths are indeed lightly entwined, and occasionally there are wild flowers which we can join to their neighbors only by an act of willful self-delusion. Wordsworth himself warns against a mechanical approach to his arrangement, explaining that it is based on several principles which he implies are not always in harmony with one another: "The most striking characteristics of each piece, mutual illustration, variety, and proportion, have governed me throughout."[1] He is speaking here mainly of classification, but the arrangement of poems within a class was determined by an equally varied set of principles. Complete success could not be expected of a plan so generous and ambitious, but it deserves more than it has had.

We may begin by noting two apparently contradictory tendencies in Wordsworth's remarks on fancy. To defend this faculty against Coleridge's unflattering description of it in an essay written for Southey's *Omniana*,[2] he categorizes fancy and imagination together when listing "the powers requisite for the production of poetry" and describes the functions of both in one phrase: "to modify, to create, and to associate." Later on he explicitly mentions Coleridge's definition of fancy as "'the aggregative and associative power'" and rejects it on the ground that these functions, as well as those of evoking and combining, are common to the two powers.[3] So much for his defense of fancy. The remainder of this section of the Preface presents a series of contrasts between the two faculties, all to the distinct disadvantage of fancy.

It is easy enough to add this apparent confusion in attitude to our list of Wordsworthian obscurities, but there is a far better way to deal with it. In the Preface and in the class "Poems of the Fancy," his basis for the defense of this

[1] *PW*, II, 434.
[2] This essay is discussed by Coleridge in *BL*, I, 193. For Coleridge's reply to Wordsworth's criticism of his definition see *BL*, I, 194.
[3] *PW*, II, 432, 441.

faculty is moral or religious, not aesthetic. He consistently writes of fancy as a power artistically inferior to imagination. But he insists upon the importance of fancy as an essential complement to the higher power: "Fancy is given to quicken and to beguile the temporal part of our nature, Imagination to incite and to support the eternal."[4] No one has described better the different *perspectives* of these two faculties. The poems of fancy have as their materials the *evidences* on earth of a universal spirit of love; in the poems of imagination Wordsworth turns to the mysterious and awful *source* of this love, which permeates the natural world but is not confined in it. These poems glance "from earth to heaven."[5]

The two classes of poems explore a single subject and a single theme, evidences of divine grace and man's receptivity to grace. The order of both classes is from simple to complex presentations of this subject and theme. The complexity, however, is not artistic but philosophical, so that we cannot expect to find the best poems near the end of each class. In fact, the arrangement of these classes in the last collection supervised by Wordsworth, the edition of 1849–1850, follows almost an order according to date of composition. The last poems of both classes are in the style and spirit of the later Wordsworth.

"To the Daisy," the introductory selection in "Poems of the Fancy," is preceded by a motto from a poem by George Wither. Together the motto and the poem define, illustrate, and justify on moral grounds the operations of fancy. In every respect "To the Daisy" is an unpretentious

[4] *PW*, II, 442.
[5] *PW*, II, 436.

poem, and this very quality makes it an appropriate introduction to the poems of fancy. De Selincourt follows
Thomas Hutchinson in attributing three of the four poems
on the daisy, three of them classified as poems of fancy in
1815, to Wordsworth's intensive study of Elizabethan
poets, and notes that Wordsworth imitates in these poems
the metre of a poem by Ben Jonson.[6] This similarity of style
is part of a more profound kinship. As a group the poems
of fancy constitute Wordsworth's nostalgic tribute to what
he took to be (and what is sometimes still assumed to have
been) a joyous, unsophisticated age, and more to the point,
an age that appeared to have a cheerful faith in the benev-
olence of Nature and in the high calling of the poet. This
Romantic view of the Elizabethans, poignantly expressed
in Keats's "Bards of Passion and of Mirth," "Lines on the
Mermaid Tavern," and the sonnet "To Spenser," surely
underlies Wordsworth's longing for

> the good old age
> When Fancy was Truth's willing Page;
> And Truth would skim the flowery glade,
> Though entering but as Fancy's Shade.[7]

Earlier in our century it was fashionable to laugh at or to
apologize for Romantic sentimentality. Today, because
serious scholars of romanticism have done their work so
well, we need to be reminded that sentimental longing for a
simpler past is as truly a part of Romantic poetry as
Shelley's "intellectual system" and the Mind of Keats. In the
works and literary personalities of Burton, Browne, and
Walton, and in some of the minor poets of the sixteenth and

[6] *PW*, II, 490.
[7] "A Flower Garden," ll. 53–56. This poem stands second in the
class of Fancy in the last collected edition supervised by Wordsworth.

early seventeenth centuries, the Romantic poets found charm and sweetness; and these two qualities are precisely those that Wordsworth emphasized in the poems of fancy.[8]

In "To the Daisy" simplicity of style reflects simplicity of faith, and the unimpressiveness of the flower is made a virtue. The basis for the restful, quietly confident tone of the poem is summed up in the motto and in the first stanza:

> Her [the Muse] divine skill taught me this,
> That from every thing I saw
> I could some instruction draw,
> And raise pleasure to the height
> Through the meanest object's sight.

and

> In youth from rock to rock I went,
> From hill to hill in discontent
> Of pleasure high and turbulent,
>   Most pleased when most uneasy;
> But now my own delights I make,—
> My thirst at every rill can slake,
> And gladly Nature's love partake
>   Of Thee, sweet Daisy!

Tone, subject, and style combine to illustrate the innocence and calm made possible by the simple faith that Nature is a harmony of pleasant images. The turbulence of youthful passions, the awful sublimity of Nature's grand objects and scenes, the thirst for "Types and Emblems of

[8] Wordsworth's fullest illustration of the charm of fancy is a lengthy quotation from Cotton's "Ode Upon Winter," a poem that he obviously, though somewhat apologetically, admired. See *PW*, II, 442–444. Charles Lamb introduced Wordsworth to this poem. See *The Letters of Charles and Mary Lamb*, ed. E. V. Lucas (London: J. M. Dent and Sons Ltd., 1935), I, 337.

Eternity"—these are desirable materials for the imagination, but have no place in poems of fancy. There are in the poems of imagination natural objects as simple as daisies and celandines, but fancy plays lightly over them while imagination transforms them into symbols of eternity. It is mainly the mood of the poet that distinguishes between these two classes of poems, and this is what Wordsworth means when he writes of the different laws under which these faculties operate.[9] The imaginative vision comes upon one unawares, and though it lives and operates in memory, it is itself a fleeting experience. The processes of fancy are capricious, by which term, oddly enough, Wordsworth means more under one's control. The effects of fancy are superficial, and though this is a weakness it is also a strength. For while the imaginative vision quickly vanishes and cannot be recalled at will, fancy "cares not how unstable or transitory may be her influence, knowing that it will not be out of her power to resume it upon an apt occasion."[10] Fancy's daisy is a "Child of the Year," and though what fancy makes of her object is neither profound nor deeply moving, it is always available to provide, promiscuously,

> Some apprehension;
> Some steady love; some brief delight;
> Some memory that had taken flight;
> Some chime of fancy wrong or right;
> Or stray invention.

The daisy's unambitious happiness is an emblem for the instruction of man. It is pleased if greeted, undaunted if not. The instruction it offers is equally unambitious, but also

[9] *PW*, II, 441.
[10] *PW*, II, 441.

equally reliable: it is available to man "all day long" and "All seasons through." This perfect accessibility is its great advantage over the grander objects and impulses of Nature.

Not all the poems of fancy are so joyful as this one. There is a progression in fact from scenes showing man in perfect harmony with simple Nature to explorations of human characteristics that threaten this natural harmony. This more sombre strain is treated lightly in the seventh through ninth poems of the class, and thereafter more seriously. Finally in the last poem the tragic possibilities of man's alienation from natural joy are faced more squarely. Despite these differences in tone, however, the poems of fancy all retreat from a full examination of man's spiritual alienation from the spontaneously joyful creatures of Nature. To turn toward heaven or infinity, as do the poems of imagination, is to experience ecstasy. But the return to earthly perspective, occasionally described but always implied in the poems of imagination, makes one feel the more intensely our finitude, and produces a state of mingled pleasure and pain that Keats describes in these lines from "On Seeing the Elgin Marbles":

> Such dim-conceived glories of the brain
>   Bring round the heart an undescribable feud;
> So do these wonders a most dizzy pain
>   That mingles Grecian grandeur with the rude
> Wasting of old Time—with a billowy main—
> A sun—a shadow of a magnitude.

Only in his poems of fancy could Wordsworth unperplex bliss from its neighbor pain, but unlike Keats he had in his system of classification a justification for refusing to choose between poetry that soothes and poetry that vexes.

There are tragic possibilities in most of his poems of imagination. They are not fully exploited, but we are sufficiently aware of them to be sensitive to the greater passion and energy of these poems. This all-important difference, the main factor in the superiority of the poems of imagination, is reflected in the difference in structural patterns between the poems of the two classes. The poems of imagination almost invariably follow the speaker from excitement to vision to a calm that is at once the result and the proof of vision. The poems of fancy exhibit no pattern so consistent or coherent as this. They begin and end in a tone very much the same, for a poem of fancy not only effects no permanent change in the constitution of her materials, but also achieves no lasting alteration of the mind of the poet or reader. Each poem of imagination presents a new acquist of knowledge; the poems of fancy have value not singly, but in combination, because they depend upon an ability to provide a steady, undramatic source of quiet pleasure and solace.

The second poem of fancy, "A Whirl-Blast from behind the hill," seems very like a poem of imagination, but, as I have explained, actually exhibits a co-operation of the two powers in which fancy exerts the decisive influence, is "*predominant* in the production" of the poem. As in "To the Daisy," Wordsworth emphasizes that feelings attached to the natural scene are purely subjective, and he sometimes seems to have shared with less imaginative men a tendency to equate the subjective and the arbitrary. The mood of almost breathless anticipation portrayed in this poem is collapsed into overt simile:

> As if with pipes and music rare
> Some Robin Good-fellow were there,

And all those leaves, in festive glee,
Were dancing to the minstrelsy.

In these concluding lines, Wordsworth shifts his glance from awe to charm, from the sublime to the beautiful. His care in limiting the implications of both this and the daisy poem is a manifestation of Wordsworth's sometimes pedantic scrupulousness that Coleridge called "minute adherence to *matter-of-fact*."[11] In these poems and in several others of this class, Wordsworth carefully distinguishes between truth to nature and poetic invention. It is as if to uphold his claim that the highest reaches of poetry are genuine steps toward the truth, he must confess that some poems, though useful as expressions of moral sentiments, speak not objective but personal—that is, subjective or psychological—truth. This feature alone is a sufficient indication of the predominance of fancy in a poem, because it admits of a dichotomy between objective reality and subjective response. No such discrimination is permitted in poems of imagination, for in these no such dualism is assumed to exist.

The motto from Wither pictures fancy as a tool of the understanding: not a faculty for disclosing or contributing to reality, but an instrument for extracting moral lessons from experiences or natural objects and tricking them out in appealing language and metre. It is entirely fitting that a writer known for "emblem" poetry should have contributed the motto for Wordsworth's poems of fancy, for many of these can appropriately be called emblem poems. There are no actual engravings accompanying them, but the words paint illustrations and their presence is so strongly felt that

[11] *BL*, II, 103.

the poems seem legends designed to explain the emblematic significance of pictures.[12] This is particularly true of "The Waterfall and the Eglantine," "The Oak and the Broom," and "To a Sexton," but all poems of fancy depend upon the reader's acceptance of a passive Nature on which the mind works. It is not at all an exaggeration to say that in the very process of creating traditional moral poems, Wordsworth violated his own higher morality by using Nature as a means, a dead body of instructive materials. If this be assumed, the tone of defiant apology, a striking feature of these poems, can be said to conceal an uncertainty not primarily of poetic method but of moral response.[13]

[12] Although she does not discuss Wordsworth's poetry, Rosemary Freeman does describe emblem poetry by means of a distinction between fancy and imagination. The emblem poet, she writes, uses "the method of fancy rather than of imagination, as Wordsworth and Coleridge were later to define the distinction," in that "he deals in fixities and definites, establishing parallel after parallel in a purely objective way" and "deduces his ideas from it [his emblem] instead of concentrating them in it. . . ." *English Emblem Books* (London: Chatto and Windus, 1948), p. 29. Wordsworth's attraction to Wither's poems was shared by Lamb, who wrote an enthusiastic essay "On the Poetical Works of George Wither" and sent to Southey a copy of Wither's *Emblems*, along with this comment: "I perfectly accord with your opinion of old Wither. Quarles is a wittier writer, but Wither lays more hold of the heart. Quarles thinks of his audience when he lectures; Wither soliloquises in company with a full heart. . . ." This is questionable literary criticism, but eloquent evidence that Wither, with more warmth than wit, was to Lamb, and presumably to Southey and Wordsworth, something of a "romantic" poet. See *The Works of Charles and Mary Lamb*, ed. E. V. Lucas (New York: G. P. Putnam's Sons, 1903), I, 181–184, and *The Letters of Charles and Mary Lamb*, ed. E. V. Lucas (London: J. M. Dent and Sons Ltd., 1935), I, 123.

[13] See, e.g., "A Morning Exercise," ll. 1–24; "To the Daisy" ("In youth . . ."), ll. 41–48; "To the Same Flower," ll. 9–16, 41–44; "Love Lies Bleeding," ll. 10–11.

The third poem, a fifteen-line adaptation of Sidney's "With how sad steps, O moon," was rewritten as a sonnet and in subsequent editions of the collected poems placed in the class of "Miscellaneous Sonnets." Though recognizably a work of fancy, the poem differs markedly from those surrounding it in the 1815 edition, whose principal subjects are flowers, leaves, and birds. Its position in the 1815 arrangement is for this reason difficult to explain, but more than others of its class it underscores an important and paradoxical distinction between the operations of fancy and imagination. Imagination, Wordsworth says, must have plastic materials that can be shaped into new creations, yet as the poems of the two classes illustrate, though fancy achieves only transient modifications of its materials, it is also more consciously controlled by the poet's will. The visible scene enters unawares into the heart of the Winander boy, and the other visionary experiences described in the poems of imagination appear when they will and mean what they will. The daisies, celandines, and other subjects of the poems of fancy are passive instruments for a deliberate process by which such meanings are extracted as satisfy a given mood of the poet. "With how sad steps," a slight enough poem, nevertheless illustrates both the use that fancy attempts to make of natural objects and its cheerful acceptance of failure. The poem opens with a very mild lament that the slow pace of the moon invites a corresponding lethargy in the poet, moves to a wish that its pace could be so accelerated as to provide an emblem of joyous energy ("Running among the clouds a Wood-nymph's race"), and concludes with a rather irrelevant acceptance of a situation that the fancy, at least this time, cannot alter: "But, Cynthia, should to Thee the palm be giv'n. / Queen both for beauty

& for majesty."[14] A slight poem, indeed, but a reminder
that Wordsworth's fancy shares with the daisy a cheerful
acceptance of whatever happens.

The next three poems ("The Green Linnet" and two
poems "To the Small Celandine") have the tone of the first
two; like these and like the poems of this class as a whole,
they calmly celebrate a mysterious animating spirit in all
creatures of Nature. The mystery of this spirit, emphasized
above all else in the poems of imagination, is subordinated
in the poems of fancy to a cheerful acceptance of whatever
is given. Or, as in "A Whirl-Blast," the mystery is at once
affirmed and denied: because the withered leaves dance
when "There's not a breeze—no breath of air—" fancy is at
liberty to invoke a sense of magic, a Robin Good-fellow
piping "music rare," but there is no attempt to hide in the
background the purely natural cause of movement, which
is after all merely the dropping of hailstones. If man feels
most the mystery and awe when he looks or listens for the
Spirit in itself, he gains quieter charms from its appearances
in unpretentious natural objects and human beings. Four
cancelled lines from "The Green Linnet" explain the reason
why. Fancy's less ambitious aims and its ability to turn any
materials to its task protect it from the constant threat of
failure that challenges the imagination. Amidst a multitude
of objects, fancy finds a multitude of subjects, none demanding precedence and none subduing the mind by its power:

> My thoughts they all by turns employ;
> A whispering Leaf is now my joy,
> And then a Bird will be the toy
>   That doth my fancy tether.

[14] My quotations of this poem are from the text of the 1815 edition,
Poems (London, 1815); hereafter cited as 1815 ed.

The bird in "To the Cuckoo" in "Poems of the Imagination" arouses excitement and awe by concealing itself from the eye of man. The green linnet, too, conceals itself by appearing to be "A Brother of the dancing leaves." But fancy makes no insistent demands, does not exert the energy required to transform observations from the senses into visionary experience.

In most of the poems of fancy, natural objects perform two distinct but related functions: they are the taking-off points for moral reflection, and also emblems of fancy and of attitudes appropriate to it—appropriate, that is, to "hearts at leisure." [15] Like fancy itself, its materials are unambitious, unassuming, and reliable. The daisy yields wisdom and quiet confidence "all day long" and "All seasons through"; the celandine, the subject of the fifth and sixth poems, is equally accessible: ". . . there's not a place, / Howsoever mean it be, / But 'tis good enough for thee."

Thus far, the poems of fancy depict Nature and mind in a harmony so complete that the characteristics of one are equally characteristics of the other. The instructions they offer are all but indistinguishable from the attributes of fancy itself. Both human faculty and natural objects perform at the heart's command "Tasks that are no tasks." [16]

The celandine is likened to "a careless Prodigal," a description that links this poem to the preceding one on the linnet, a bird "Scattering . . . gladness without care," and to the seventh and eighth poems, two moral fables, "The Waterfall and the Eglantine" and "The Oak and the Broom." In these last two poems, one of them appropriately assigned to a rustic narrator, Wordsworth first introduces

[15] "To the Daisy" ("In youth . . ."), l. 56.
[16] "To the Small Celandine," l. 62.

the chief antagonist appearing in the poems of fancy. In the two fables it is explicitly identified as pride, but in later poems of the class it is the source of pride, the self-consciousness and rationality that belong to maturity. As Wordsworth explores this darker aspect of his theme, we understand that the poems of fancy are much like prayers that this faculty can restore in man's maturity the spontaneous joy and trust characteristic of Nature's simple creatures, natural and human—flowers and birds, children and rustics.

The eglantine and broom are emblems of innocence. Their speeches express the major themes and moral messages of the poems of fancy, above all the belief that "'he is oft the wisest man, / Who is not wise at all.'" Little creatures are contrasted with those that are "tyrannous and strong." The eglantine is swept away by the flood, the broom outlives the boasting oak, but whatever its fate the faith of each humble creature is sound. Clearly this is what Wordsworth wishes to indicate, for in "The Redbreast Chasing the Butterfly," which comes next, he makes to the proud robin the same plea for love and brotherhood uttered by the humble creatures of his fables. The light hints of disharmony in these poems echo more strongly in several that follow. Preceding them come two more poems on the daisy, "overflowings of the mind in composing the one which stands first in this Class," but placed where they will provide a modulation to the more sombre tone of the remaining poems. They are in themselves joyful, but because they follow three poems that pit trust against prideful distrust of Providence, Wordsworth's praises of the daisy remind us of man's lack of its qualities, and its secure happiness is contrasted with man's tenuous joy. The contrast is explicit in the second of these poems on the daisy, "Bright Flower! whose home is everywhere":

> Is it that Man is soon deprest?
> A thoughtless Thing! who, once unblest,
> Does little on his memory rest,
>   Or on his reason,
> And Thou wouldst teach him how to find
> A shelter under every wind,
> A hope for times that are unkind
>   And every season?

The daisy's "home is everywhere, / Bold in maternal Nature's care"; it is "Unchecked by pride or scrupulous doubt . . . / Meek, yielding to the occasion's call, / And all things suffering from all." These are the characteristics that Wordsworth values for man, but adults often lack them, and even if they have them feel they are constantly threatened. The poems that follow explore the reasons for, and the results of, man's unique and, in this instance, unenviable place in Nature. In fact, cause and result are one—man's incapacity for feeling "at home" in the natural world. Wordsworth's favorite technical device for expressing this theme, a device not characteristic of the poems of the imagination, is a contrast between natural and unnatural responses to the spirit of love in all things; and unnatural, in these poems, almost always means "rational." Thus, in the next poem, "To a Sky-Lark," the bird's instinctive joy is set against weary man, who must earn his joy by conscious effort. The bird is "Joyous as morning" and its joy is as inevitable as morning. It is joyful because it is completely at home in the natural world ("Thou hast a nest for thy love and thy rest"). The speaker's joy is evanescent, and a more permanent joy must be postponed from this world to the next. Even this permanent joy is in some doubt: he will "hope for higher raptures, when life's day is done." The bird's flight is free and, in the best sense, aimless, for any place is home. Bound to earth yet building his hope on the prospect of heaven, man is embarked on a "journey, rugged and uneven, / Through prickly moors or dusty ways."

The next two poems are complementary studies of man's unique position. "To a Sexton" is about human death, but more specifically about the uniquely human awareness of mortality that separates man from all other creatures, man alone being born for death. The next poem, "Who fancied what a pretty sight," provides a counterpoise for the sombre tone of the first one. If death is ever present, so are divine love and purpose. A rock "edged around / With living snow-drops" forms a pattern arguing conscious design; reducing all rational explanations of that design to the status of efficient cause, Wordsworth looks to the Cause beyond causes, that chooses to reveal itself in objects of quiet, unassuming beauty: "the Spirit of Paradise . . . / That gives to all the self-same bent / Where life is wise and innocent."

The next poem, "Song for the Wandering Jew," might more properly have followed "To a Sky-Lark," for the theme and imagery are very similar. In one sense the Jew's experience is unique, for he has rejected grace in its very incarnation; but his experience is Everyman's. In its general application, the "Song" is a more pessimistic portrait of the man of "To a Sky-Lark," alienated from Nature and pursuing a rugged and uncertain journey. The first six stanzas of "Song" present six images of unconscious harmony with Nature. The mountain torrents, the clouds, the chamois, the sea-horse, the raven, and the ostrich are completely at home in the world; all have their "Resting-places calm and deep." The final stanza reveals the sad consequence of man's inability to find this natural repose:

> Day and night my toils redouble,
> Never nearer to the goal;
> Night and day, I feel the trouble
> Of the Wanderer in my soul.

The Jew of legend rejects love because of pride and hatred, unnatural emotions that Wordsworth attributed only to man of all Nature's creatures. Another unnatural emotion is the subject of the poem that follows, "The Seven Sisters." In the poems of fancy so far discussed divine love is expressed through natural objects. In the last five poems of the class Wordsworth turns to the other chief repositories of this love, infants, children, and youths, who share the spontaneous joy and perfect trust of natural things. As the Wandering Jew turns aside from Love incarnate in Christ, so the father of the seven sisters spurns the natural love of his daughters for a perversion of love ("He loved the Wars so well").

The last four poems are cogent evidence that Wordsworth successfully carried out the plan described in the letter of 1809, "that there should be a scale in each class" of his poems. In these final poems there is no change of theme, but this theme asserts itself so powerfully that it is no longer depreciated, as it was in the earlier poems, by the framework that embodies it. The result is better poetry, in which subject and theme are more intimately related, with no distracting dichotomy between "story" and "message." Two lines from the next poem, "Stray Pleasures," can serve as a suitable motto for the poems of fancy. Wordsworth himself thought them important enough to use them as a summary of the theme of the poem: "Pleasure is spread through the earth / In stray gifts to be claimed by whoever shall find." Change the *shall* to *will* and the lines state succinctly the creed of all the poems of fancy. A loving Providence has ordained that love is the law of Nature, but to live by this law demands from man cheerful willingness to submit to it. If he does not, like the father of the seven sisters and like the Wandering Jew, he lives unnaturally, alienated from this law. The miller and "two Dames" of "Stray Pleasures" are in a position to receive these gifts of pleasure. They do not question Providence, nor do they seek to escape the roles it has designed for them. Instead, "They from morning to even take whatever is given."

In this poem and the two that follow, Wordsworth is careful to emphasize that joy is a law of Nature, spontaneous and unconscious in its simpler creatures, and that it is best received spontaneously and unconsciously. The music that sets to dancing the inhabitants of the mill is not only not of their own making, but is not expressly intended for them:

> It plays not for them,—what matter? 'tis theirs;
> And if they had care, it has scattered their cares
> While they dance, crying, "Long as ye please!"

His acceptance of this same attitude, grateful response to a gift whose origin and duration one has no right to question, enables the speaker of the poem to share in it—

> They dance not for me,
> Yet mine is their glee!—

and to gain insight into the source and nature of this gift, an insight compressed into the motto of the poem. The poem ends with an expression of the unwavering faith in Providence that pervades the poems of fancy:

> The showers of the spring
> Rouse the birds, and they sing;
> If the wind do but stir for his proper delight,
> Each leaf, that and this, his neighbour will kiss;
> Each wave, one and t'other, speeds after his brother;
> They are happy, for that is their right!

This, then, is the theme of these poems: happiness, a gift of Nature, is not only to be found, but will almost inevitably be found, for the production of joy is inevitable. One thing, however, can obstruct the natural course of joy in its inundation of all the universe, and that one thing is a willful refusal to accept these gifts that Nature everywhere offers. The only one of Nature's creatures that habitually refuses to accept these gifts is man, and the contrast between the meek and thoughtless compliance of Nature's simpler creatures and the recalcitrance of man, an important underlying strain in all the poems of fancy, is the major theme of the concluding poems—"The Kitten and Falling Leaves," "The Danish Boy," and "Address to my Infant Daughter, Dora." In all three poems there is a contrast between the spontaneous joy of children and the melancholy of adults, whose faith in loving Providence has been subjected to disappointment and despair, because having lost this innate trust in Nature they have lost as well their power to correct the despondency that human misdeeds have created in them. The highly developed consciousness of the mature adult has robbed him of the most precious of Nature's gifts:

> ... whate'er enjoyments dwell
> In the impenetrable cell

Of the silent heart which Nature
Furnishes to every creature;
Whatsoe'er we feel and know
Too sedate for outward show,
Such a light of gladness breaks,
Pretty Kitten! from thy freaks,—
Spreads with such a living grace
O'er my little Dora's face;
Yes, the sight so stirs and charms
Thee, Baby, laughing in my arms,
That almost I could repine
That your transports are not mine,
That I do not wholly fare
Even as ye do, thoughtless pair!

This example of spontaneous joy is something man must strive to imitate, but his being forced to *strive* for spontaneity is an ironic reminder that his quest can never be wholly successful:

And I will have my careless season
Spite of melancholy reason,
Will walk through life in such a way
That, when time brings on decay,
Now and then I may possess
Hours of perfect gladsomeness.

Nowhere is Wordsworth's persistent anti-rationalism more apparent. Because he has learned to associate reason with the vexing moral problems that bring on despair, the adult can never hope to regain completely the "perfect gladsomeness" that was his in childhood. When he does regain something akin to that innocent and unconscious joy, he can regain it only for "hours" and only "now and then." And he can regain it only because "in our embers / Is

something that doth live, / That nature yet *remembers*."
The gift which the kitten and the infant have that the adult
speaker of the poem has not is "that which is most worthy to
be blest; / Delight and liberty, the simple creed / Of
Childhood"—and, Wordsworth would certainly add, of all
Nature's creatures who respond to her gift of joy with
unquestioning acceptance.[17] Both this poem and "Stray
Pleasures" emphasize that in order to share in Nature's gift
of joy, man must turn his back on "melancholy reason" and
learn again "To gambol with Life's falling Leaf."

The position of the next poem, "The Danish Boy,"
appears at first a vexing problem. There is no doubt that
its theme is that of the two poems just discussed, but since
the last poem in this class is much closer in tone to "Stray
Pleasures" and "The Kitten and Falling Leaves," "The
Danish Boy" seems an interruption. Perhaps because he
realized this, Wordsworth later placed the poem so that in
the 1849–1850 edition it immediately precedes the "Song
for the Wandering Jew" and provides a striking contrast
between the alienation of the Jew and the serenity of the
young boy, who is said to be "blest / And happy in his
flowery cove." It is possible, however, to justify the position
of this poem in the 1815 plan, for its hero shares with the
infant Dora of the preceding and following poems a
thoughtless harmony with Nature. Throughout the poem
Wordsworth emphasizes this harmony (in a manner quite
similar to that employed in "Lucy Gray") by transforming
the boy into "A Spirit of noon-day" and by consistently
describing him in imagery suggesting objects and processes
of Nature. He wears a "vest of fur . . . / In colour like a

[17] Quotations from the "Intimations Ode," ll. 130–132, 136–138.
Italics mine.

raven's wing," which "in the storm . . . [is] fresh and blue /
As budding pines in spring"; and "His helmet has a vernal
grace, / Fresh as the bloom upon his face." In the very
subtle concluding passage of the poem, Wordsworth draws
his striking contrast between the mental attitudes of youth
and maturity. Half of this contrast is not stated, but implicit
is his belief that man's greater powers of reasoning often—
perhaps always—are a burden to him. To the adult, war is
an evil which his reason can discern but never explain, and
for which it can offer no solace. But this is not true of youth:

> The lovely Danish Boy is blest
> And happy in his flowery cove:
> From bloody deeds his thoughts are far;
> And yet he warbles songs of war,
> *That seem like songs of love.*[18]

Of the concluding poem of fancy Wordsworth wrote in
the Preface of 1815: ". . . 'An address to an Infant' . . . exhibits something of this communion and interchange of
instruments and functions between the two powers [fancy
and imagination]; and is, accordingly, placed last in the class,
as a preparation for that of Imagination which follows."[19]
The theme and modulations of tone in the "Address"
reveal its kinship with "The Kitten and Falling Leaves" and
even more with the "Intimations Ode." It is, moreover, as
Wordsworth explained, a preparation for his poems of
imagination, not only because it is far superior to almost all
others of its class, but also because its use of imagery closely
approximates the activities of imagination as he describes
them in the Preface of 1815. The moon-infant image

[18] Italics mine.
[19] *PW*, II, 442.

depends "less upon outline of form and feature, than upon expression and effect" and its modifications are not so "slight, limited, and evanescent" as those of the fancy.[20] Nevertheless, we can discern the presence of fancy in his labelling the image an "Apt likeness," a self-conscious confession, characteristic only of the poems of fancy, that he is indeed employing an artistic image, not spontaneous but one of his "Apt illustrations of the moral world, / . . . traced with curious pains."[21]

This poem divides into four parts. It opens in a mood reminiscent of what is now called Jacobean melancholy and on a theme that we associate most often with the writers of that period, mutability and the decay of the world:

> Hast thou then survived—
> Mild Offspring of infirm humanity,
> Meek Infant! among all forlornest things
> The most forlorn—one life of that bright star,
> The second glory of the Heavens?—Thou hast;
> Already hast survived that great decay,
> That transformation through the wide earth felt,
> And by all nations.

His daughter's having survived "one life" of the moon makes available to Wordsworth the traditional association of the moon with mutability and perpetual decay, a device he would have known very well from the works of Spenser. In the next lines, however, this image undergoes a transformation. Wordsworth first rejects the moon as an appropriate image with which to compare human existence: "But what is time? What outward glory? Neither / A

[20] *PW*, II, 441.
[21] *Prelude*, XIV, 319–320.

measure is of Thee, whose claims extend / Through 'heaven's eternal year.'" The changes of the moon record time only quantitatively; there is no place in its calculations for distinctly human attitudes toward time, made possible by man's faith that the life of his soul is something beyond time as it is measured by physical phenomena.[22] Instead, for men of such faith,

> Mother's love,
> Nor less than mother's love in other breasts,
> Will, among us warm-clad and warmly housed,
> Do for thee what the finger of the heavens
> Doth all too often harshly execute
> For thy unblest coevals ....

This fairly cheerful tone is sustained in the next few lines. The moon is seen now less as an image of decay than as an "apt likeness" to the infant girl. The moon's "Moving untouched in silver purity" is likened to the infant's "sinless progress, through a world / By sorrow darkened and by care disturbed." It is the purity of the moon—and no doubt its mythological associations with chastity—that Wordsworth now emphasizes, and its mutability is seen less as likeness than as contrast to the infant's life:

> But thou, how leisurely thou fill'st thy horn
> With brightness! leaving her to post along,
> And range about, disquieted in change,
> And still impatient of the shape she wears.
> Once up, once down the hill, one journey, Babe,

[22] Wordsworth implies that for people of a primitive culture, only physical measurements of time were possible, because savages lacked the confidence in immortality developed in civilized societies. In this poem as in "Ruth" there is no Rousseauistic admiration of noble savages.

> That will suffice thee; and it seems that now
> Thou hast foreknowledge that such task is thine;
> Thou travellest so contentedly, and sleep'st
> In such a heedless peace.

At this point, however, the tone suddenly changes. The roles of moon and infant are reversed, and now it is the moon that moves contentedly and the child who seems disquieted:

> Alas! full soon
> Hath this conception, grateful to behold,
> Changed countenance, like an object sullied o'er
> By breathing mist; and thine appears to be
> A mournful labour, while to her is given
> Hope, and a renovation without end.

The conception changes countenance because Wordsworth has introduced his recurrent theme of man's progressive separation from the unconscious life of Nature. The moon seems to have hope because as an unconscious and inseparable part of Nature its progress is in the strict sense never altered. The infant, whose growing powers of "melancholy reason" will too soon obscure the unity of all creation, will find life "A mournful labour."

But, as in most of the poems of fancy, this melancholy tone is not final. The unconscious joy of a child performs a function similar to that of the "timely utterance" in the great Ode, and the poem can come to rest on a note of faith:

> —That smile forbids the thought; for on thy face
> Smiles are beginning, like the beams of dawn,
> To shoot and circulate; smiles have there been seen,—
> Tranquil assurances that Heaven supports
> The feeble motions of thy life, and cheers

Thy loneliness: or shall those smiles be called
Feelers of love, put forth as if to explore
This untried world, and to prepare thy way
Through a strait passage intricate and dim?
Such are they; and the same are tokens, signs,
Which, when the appointed season hath arrived,
Joy, as her holiest language, shall adopt;
And Reason's godlike Power be proud to own.

This appointed season, there can be little doubt, is that of the
"years that bring the philosophic mind." The unconscious
joy lost, its place will be filled by the *rational* faith (to
Wordsworth this phrase would not embody a contradiction)
that man's soul has the unity and continuity of a rainbow,
so that these original impulses of unconscious joy are
transformed rather than lost.

While admitting that Wordsworth himself was tempted
to dismiss fancy as a playful faculty, we should also recognize that its very playfulness has the charm of childhood
innocence. And remembering the value Wordsworth
placed on that condition, we need not wonder that he could
cleave to his conception of fancy as if it were an article of
faith, for in fact it was. True, for the sober and rational
"keepers of our time, / The guides and wardens of our
faculties"—and, alas, even for Coleridge—the reputation
of fancy suffered from the peculiarly Anglo-Saxon guilt
that lingers about indulgent pleasure. But Wordsworth
gave his reply to such men, half seriously in "The Tables
Turned" and earnestly in *The Prelude*:

When will their presumption learn,
That in the unreasoning progress of the world
A wiser spirit is at work for us,

A better eye than theirs, most prodigal
Of blessings, and most studious of our good,
Even in what seem our most unfruitful hours?

(V, 353–363)

"Wise passiveness" is the way of fancy. It is no substitute for the higher, more intense power of imagination, but it provides a profitable means for filling the intervals between the infrequent visitations of mystical vision. And even though Wordsworth believed that fancy can be willed into action and imagination cannot, he also believed, consistently or not, that the mild and relaxed mode of fancy is a response to that same mood in Nature. For if Nature has two moods so must the human mind have attitudes appropriate to each. This was the great lesson of Wordsworth's maturity that helped to restore his imagination:

From Nature doth emotion come, and moods
Of calmness equally are Nature's gift:
This is her glory; these two attributes
Are sister horns that constitute her strength.
Hence Genius, born to thrive by interchange
Of peace and excitation, finds in her
His best and purest friend; from her receives
That energy by which he seeks the truth,
From her that happy stillness of the mind
Which fits him to receive it when unsought.

(*Prelude*, XIII, 1–10)

Energy and stillness—these are the responses that Nature both demands and makes possible. For Wordsworth, these are also the terms by which the activities of fancy and imagination are to be defined. The poems of fancy are his memorials to the second of these responses.

Wordsworth made far fewer changes in the arrangement of "Poems of the Imagination" than in that of "Poems of the Fancy," and while he wrote nothing specifically about the order of poems of fancy, he did discuss in the Preface the order of the poems of imagination. But for all this, the pattern that emerges from the order of the poems of fancy is by far the more lucid and coherent. The movement in both classes is from particular to general experiences and from implication to explicit statement of theme. The most obvious difference between the two arrangements is a difference between static and dynamic pictures. Most poems in both classes present reflections of an adult speaker on attributes especially characteristic of children. But in the poems of fancy these characteristics are found exclusively either in natural objects or in infants and children not identified with the speaker, while in the poems of imagination the experiences are the speaker's own memories of various stages of his life. Only this class, therefore, traces the growth of a poet's mind. In the poems of fancy the subject is the *product* of this growth, a quality already existent, "the calm existence" of maturity made possible by that growth. Furthermore in all but a few of the poems of imagination reflection on experiences is consistently subordinated to the experiences themselves. Hence the drama in the better poems and the sense of framed paintings in the poems of fancy.

In the plan considered by Wordsworth in 1809, "There Was a Boy," which in all collected editions of the poems stands first in the class "Poems of the Imagination," was to come just before the "Intimations Ode" at the end of those poems "relating to childhood, and such feelings as rise in the mind in after life in direct contemplation of that state." Wordsworth's probable reason for shifting the position of this poem is not difficult to discern. "There Was a Boy" fits perfectly the description of that group of poems which later formed the basis for both the poems of the imagination and of the fancy: "Poems relating to natural objects and their influence on the mind either as growing or in an advanced state." Wordsworth's explanation of the order of the poems of imagination in the 1815 edition is an elaboration of the plan of 1809:

> ... in the series of Poems placed under the head of Imagination, I have begun with one of the earliest processes of Nature in the development of this faculty. Guided by one of my own primary consciousnesses, I have presented a commutation and transfer of internal feelings, co-operating with external accidents, to plant, for immortality, images of sound and sight, in the celestial soil of the Imagination. ... The Poems next in succession exhibit the faculty exerting itself upon various objects of the external universe; then follow others, where it is employed upon feelings, characters, and actions; and the Class is concluded with imaginative pictures of moral, political and religious sentiments.[23]

As a very general outline of the arrangement Wordsworth's comment is helpful, but anyone who applies it to the position of particular poems will likely feel that it promises more than it delivers. Nevertheless, there is in the order of these poems a familiar Wordsworthian scheme—sensation and childhood, affections and youth, reflections and maturity. However one may question the reason for the positions of individual poems, the ages of man is a unifying

[23] *PW*, II, 440.

principle lending at least a measure of coherence to the class as a whole.

The five poems that follow "There Was a Boy" were meant to show the imagination "exerting itself upon various objects of the external universe." Four of the five share with the introductory poem a mode of symbolism peculiarly characteristic of the poems of imagination, whereby a natural object or scene is endowed with meaning that cannot be reduced to rational concepts. Each poem relates an experience in which the visible scene suddenly affords a glimpse of the ultimate reality that it normally conceals, in which the burden of the mystery of the visible world gives way to a recognition of the soul's participation in a reality transcending time and space.

"To the Cuckoo," like "There Was a Boy," relates an experience in which the senses are first strained to their limits in an attempt to locate a sound, and then suddenly frustrated, with an effect that Wordsworth once described to De Quincey:

> I have remarked, from my earliest days, that if, under any circumstances, the attention is energetically braced up to an act of steady observation, or of steady expectation, then, if this intense condition of vigilance should suddenly relax, at that moment any beautiful, any impressive visual object, or collection of objects, falling upon the eye, is carried to the heart with a power not known under other circumstances.[24]

The first three poems of imagination are the results of experiences similar to this one, two triggered by an image of sound, the other by an image of sight. The circumstance

[24] Thomas De Quincey, *Literary Reminiscences* (Boston, 1882), p. 314.

of this experience in "To the Cuckoo" is less dramatic than
that of the other two, but is nevertheless, like them, a
description of a situation in which the senses are frustrated:

> . . . that Cry
> Which made me look a thousand ways
> In bush, and tree, and sky.
>
> To seek thee did I often rove
> Through woods and on the green;
> And thou wert still a hope, a love;
> Still longed for, never seen.

The visionary experience described in "There Was a Boy,"
though it is an experience that recurs, shares with that of the
third poem, "A Night-Piece," a suddenness of revelation:

> Then, sometimes, in that silence, while he hung
> Listening, a gentle shock of mild surprise
> Has carried far into his heart the voice
> Of mountain-torrents . . . .

The traveller of "A Night-Piece" does not look up, because
"The sky is overcast / With a continuous cloud of texture
close," but suddenly the scene to which his eyes have
become accustomed is radically altered and its familiarity
taken away:

> At length a pleasant instantaneous gleam
> Startles the pensive traveller while he treads
> His lonesome path, with unobserving eye
> Bent earthwards; he looks up—the clouds are split
> Asunder,—and above his head he sees
> The clear Moon, and the glory of the heavens.

And just as in the first poem, this state of excitement is
succeeded by a calm that accompanies revelation:

> At length the Vision closes; and the mind,
> Not undisturbed by the delight it feels,

Which slowly settles into peaceful calm,
Is left to muse upon the solemn scene.

De Quincey tells of a similar experience when he and Wordsworth were waiting expectantly for the arrival of a mail coach, at a time of such darkness as that described in "A Night-Piece":

> At intervals, Wordsworth had stretched himself at length on the high road, applying his ear to the ground, so as to catch any sound of wheels that might be groaning along at a distance. Once, when he was slowly rising from this effort, his eye caught a bright star that was glittering between the brow of Seat Sandal, and of the mighty Helvellyn.[25]

According to De Quincey, it was this experience that led Wordsworth to discuss the incident related in "There Was a Boy," but it is applicable as well to all those poems describing scenes of hushed expectation and sudden vision.

Many of Wordsworth's poems employ memory and imagination as both subject and theme, but it would be difficult to find better brief examples than these first three poems of imagination.[26] Their full meaning for Wordsworth is contained in the matrix of past and present experience, the encounter of permanent objects of Nature and a persisting human identity. The effect of his technique in these poems is to break down the usual barriers ascribed to time and change by assigning to youthful and adult stages of life roles in a process that is single and timeless, the growth of the mind.

[25] *Ibid.*
[26] On Wordsworth's uses of memory see a recent study by Christopher Salvesen, *The Landscape of Memory: A Study of Wordsworth's Poetry* (Lincoln: University of Nebraska Press, 1965).

Even without the aid of an earlier draft of "There Was a Boy" identifying the Winander boy with Wordsworth, it would be clear that the boy's death and the speaker's mourning of it are equally facts about Wordsworth himself.[27] The boy is Wordsworth as a boy, now become the symbolical representation of a power that seems locked in the past.

There are two likely responses to the loss of childhood vision, and these three poems incorporate both, just as do "Tintern Abbey," the "Intimations Ode," and "Peele Castle." In fact, the history of Wordsworth's declining faith can be read as the stages by which his pessimistic attitude toward the change from infancy to maturity by degrees eclipsed, or anyway subdued, the optimistic one. Of the first three poems of imagination, "There Was a Boy" is the most elegiac in tone and "To the Cuckoo," the most joyful. Yet all three partake of both tones and the theme of each is the same: the spiritual relationship between the commonplace and visionary and the extent to which the first is transformed and re-interpreted by means of the second.

Even readers not critical of the last stanza of "There Was a Boy" are likely to concede that it is somehow an appendage, perhaps an epilogue, to the poem proper. Although in a sense it is an epilogue, it is more closely woven into the poem than has usually been recognized. Wordsworth's explanation of the poem, previously quoted, puts the emphasis on the future of the boy's experience, its residence in memory and its transformation by the mature imagination. So, in fact, does the poem. The "visible scene" that enters "unawares" is contrasted carefully with the mind

[27] For the earlier draft of the poem see *Prelude*, pp. 639–640.

into which it enters. The setting is at first a multitude of discrete images—rocks, woods, sky—unorganized and inchoate, only the raw materials of mystical vision. It becomes unified, hence becomes meaningful in human terms, when it is received "Into the bosom of the steady lake." The images in poems of imagination almost never admit of allegorical interpretation, but the steady lake can certainly be identified with memory. Until the boy's separate and distinct sensations are composed by the imagination into a unity, a *scene*, they cannot be implanted in memory for future use by the imagination. Like facts for Keats, images are not truths for imagination until they have been proved upon the pulses, until, that is, they have been shaped into unity and invested with human meaning. Far from being a mere addition to the poem, the concluding stanza is a testament to the value of the boy's experience, as it is also Wordsworth's poetic statement of the operations of both the primary and the secondary imagination. In Kantian (and Coleridgean) terms, the primary imagination fuses the welter of sensations into a unit, a "sensuous manifold," working unconsciously, "unawares." The secondary imagination, the poetic faculty, enriches the original experience that has been fixed in memory. Because it can be strengthened so as to become an habitual activity, the secondary imagination is at once spontaneous and yet conscious and volitional.[28] The man standing mute over the symbolic representation of his past is proof that childhood sensation and feeling have become adult values. That the first part of the poem is better poetry is undeniable, but aesthetically complete though it is, it is not the whole poem

[28] See *BL*, I, 202. The term "sensuous manifold" is of course Kant's.

for Wordsworth. The vast universe has converged on a single small point and has become "A firmament reflected in a sea."[29] So it is when "the Infinite Being accommodates himself to a finite capacity"—to human imagination and memory. This Being accommodates itself, Wordsworth writes in 1815, by means of symbols, and the two parts of "There Was a Boy" constitute one of Wordsworth's poetic affirmations of this creed.[30]

The same belief informs the other two poems. In "To the Cuckoo" we meet again the creative uses of memory. The sound of the bird, its disembodied voice, is not, as are physical things, of one time or one place. To recognize, as the speaker does, that the invisible voice he hears is the same as the one heard in childhood is an intimation of immortality. The human mind is in essence unchanging, its earlier stages renewable in memory. With that renewal comes the power of wonder that sometimes seems to have been buried in childhood. Nothing is lost to memory and imagination, and we can "beget / That golden time again," so that "the earth we pace / Again appears to be / An unsubstantial, faery place," not unresisting and solid, but plastic under the power of the human mind. "A Night-Piece" is a variation on this theme. There is no mention of childhood or of a repeated specific experience, but childhood is present nonetheless. It reveals itself here in the tone of the adult traveller whose rapt speech is the language of mystics, and of children—". . . how fast they [the stars] wheel away, / Yet vanish not!—the wind is in the tree, / But they are silent." This silence is no ordinary fact of perception, but

[29] Keats, *Endymion*, I, 300. Cf. Shelley, *Prometheus Unbound*, IV, 382–384, where regenerated Man is described as "a sea reflecting love."

[30] *PW*, II, 412.

an emergence of that propensity to mysticism that a man owes to his childhood. It is the tone of awe and expectation that gives to Coleridge's "Frost at Midnight" its special and elusive charm—"The frost performs its silent ministry / Unhelped by any wind." We know what can be made of such statements when they are divested of their proper tone and context. The practice of doing so was a favorite occupation of Wordsworth's reviewers. But "A Night-Piece" and the other two poems are evidence of Wordsworth's (and for a shorter time, Coleridge's) faith that no images and no experiences are ordinary unless one stubbornly wills them to be.

The next three poems in the class ("Yew-Trees," "View from the Top of Black Comb," and "Nutting") also describe visionary glimpses, but the visions of these poems are more explicitly ascribed to spiritual revelation and thus represent a more advanced stage of the mind in its exertions upon external objects. The first three make no attempt to explain the experiences they describe, whereas, in varying degree, the next three do. Two of these, "Yew-Trees" and "Nutting," are perhaps the clearest expressions we have of what is sometimes called Wordsworth's animism. In the first, the trees are said to be living things not "uninformed with Phantasy, and looks / That threaten the profane"; and though Wordsworth's personifications may at first appear conventional enough, they are less artistic devices than attempts to characterize the qualities of life these natural objects seem really to possess. In "Nutting" he implies that the trees can feel the effects of the boy's cruel ravage of them, and a belief that "there is a spirit in the woods" underlies both poems.[31]

[31] Many readers of H. W. Piper's *The Active Universe* (London: University of London, Athlone Press, 1962) have felt that his case for

In the second group of the class the principal subjects are human beings rather than inanimate objects—a logical progression if we remember that Wordsworth's overall aim in his arrangement was to show the growth of imagination, as it was first quickened by natural objects and later applied to man and his affections. Since he maintained that his love of Nature led to love of man, it is appropriate that his poems dealing with the exertion of imagination on natural objects should be followed with poems on the subject of love. The first of these, "She was a Phantom of delight," is eminently suited to its position in the arrangement, for in it Wordsworth traces in miniature the growth of the mind in its responses to love. Each of the three stanzas of the poem represents a stage in the process of this growth. In the first, the object of love is not seen as a woman at all. Instead she is a "phantom," an "apparition," a "dancing shape," and an "image"; she is presented in the metaphor of a natural phenomenon, a will-of-the-wisp, and described entirely in words suggesting natural objects and processes:

> Her eyes as stars of Twilight fair;
> Like Twilight's, too, her dusky hair;
> But all things else about her drawn
> From May-time and the cheerful Dawn.

The second stanza presents the heroine in a "nearer view"—

Wordsworth's pantheism is overstated. It is perhaps best to leave the question unresolved, for Wordsworth himself did not resolve it. Consider the hesitation and equivocation in the following extracts from *The Prelude*: "Coercing all things into sympathy, / To unorganic natures were transferred / My own enjoyments, or the power of truth / Coming in revelation, did converse / With things that really are . . . (II, 390–394); "To every natural form, rock, fruit, or flower, / Even the loose stones that cover the high-way, / I gave a moral life; I saw them feel, / Or linked them to some feeling . . ." (III, 130–133).

a nearer and, almost certainly, a maturer view. Now she is
neither woman nor spirit but both, "A Spirit, yet a Woman
too"; but though this is true, she is given in this stanza
distinctly human attributes, those of a woman just reaching
maturity. And so the imagery of this intermediate stanza
hovers between description of a real woman of flesh and
blood and of a spirit of Nature. Between the second and
last stanzas, obviously some time has passed, for the speaker
sees now "with eye serene / The very pulse of the machine."
And what he now sees are not virtues of a spirit of Nature
or of a spirit-woman, but of a woman endowed with
spiritual attributes:

> A Being breathing thoughtful breath,
> A Traveller between life and death;
> The reason firm, the temperate will,
> Endurance, foresight, strength, and skill;
> A perfect Woman, nobly planned,
> To warn, to comfort, and command.

In this final view, though she is "yet a Spirit still, and bright /
With something of angelic light," the angelic light lies in
the real woman's possession of distinctly human virtues.[32]

The other three poems of this group are also about love
and its effects. In the poem on the nightingale ("O
Nightingale! thou surely art") Wordsworth states his
preference for the love song of the dove over that of the
nightingale, on grounds we should expect. The nightingale's
song is one of "Tumultuous harmony and fierce," a contrast
to the stock-dove's song of "quiet blending, / Slow to
begin, and never ending; / Of serious faith, and inward

[32] For a contrasting interpretation see Walter Houghton, "Wordsworth's 'She Was a Phantom of Delight,'" *Explicator*, III, No. 3
(1944), 20.

glee." It is this serious and inward joy that Wordsworth celebrates in all his poetry, often to the distress of those critics who fail to see that his depreciation of sensual love (represented in this poem by the nightingale) is of a piece with his deepest feelings concerning man's relationship to eternity. The quieter love is preferred because in its very tranquillity Wordsworth sensed a permanence not to be found in emotions that all too soon are spent. This same quality, something "Slow to begin, and never ending," lends a significance to the song of the solitary reaper and the greeting of the Highland girl that Wordsworth could never attribute to objects or events that expend their energies in violent action. He would turn rather to "certain inherent and indestructible qualities of the human mind, and . . . the great and permanent objects that act upon it, which are equally inherent and indestructible."[33]

The last two poems of this group, the two short lyrics on the death of Lucy, also concern a kind of love, and although their meaning is far from clear, Wordsworth presumably placed them at the end of his imaginative poems on love because in Lucy Nature and human figure come together in a closeness that is almost identity; and this closeness with Nature is achieved, as always in Wordsworth's poetry, by the mediation of love. The discipline of Nature is given to Lucy as an act of love—

> "Myself will to my darling be
> Both law and impulse . . ."—

and in this communion with Nature the girl achieves a permanence beyond human attainment:

> "And her's shall be the breathing balm,
> And her's the silence and the calm
> Of mute insensate things."

[33] *PW*, II, 389.

But in the companion poem, "A Slumber did my spirit seal," we learn the peculiar character of this permanence:

> No motion has she now, no force;
> She neither hears nor sees;
> Rolled round in earth's diurnal course,
>   With rocks, and stones, and trees.

Lucy has achieved the permanence of Nature by becoming herself a part of the natural process, by losing, in fact, every distinctly human quality. The paradox that these poems force upon us is perhaps impossible to reconcile without recourse to biography and psychology.

That Wordsworth considered these lyrics to be poems about love is clear from the arrangement sketched in the letter of 1809, in which the poems "about Lucy" were to belong to the class of poems which "would relate to the fraternal affections, to friendship and to love and to all those emotions, which follow after childhood, in youth and early manhood," and in the letter they are placed just before "She was a Phantom of delight."[34] That both these poems on love end with an account of the death of the loved one is perhaps a fact which the psychological critics have a valid right to pursue, especially if Coleridge was correct in assuming that at least one of the Lucy poems was inspired by a morbid nightmare in which Wordsworth envisioned the death of his sister.[35] In any event, it is difficult to accept wholeheartedly one popular view that "Three years she grew" presents "an ideal picture of what normal human development might be, in which both the law and the impulse, the kindling and restraining power of nature

[34] *MY*, I, 307.
[35] *Collected Letters of Samuel Taylor Coleridge*, ed. Earl Leslie Griggs (Oxford: Oxford University Press, 1956–1959), I, 479.

lead to the perfect development of beauty and grace."[36]
Such an interpretation might well be applicable to all but the
last stanza of the poem, but this conclusion and the sequel
poem cannot but make us wonder that the inevitable result
of Nature's influence is death—and a death that cancels out
all human traits and features. The dramatic juxtaposition
of the first and third lines of the last stanza of "Three years
she grew" is terrible in its implication: the "work" that
Nature has done is, in fact, the death of the child she had
adopted, And the promise that Lucy's will be "the silence
and the calm / Of mute insensate things" is tragically fulfilled in the last stanza of the companion poem. It is by
virtue of their theme, then, and not of their tone, that these
lyrics belong where Wordsworth placed them, for it is theme
alone that they share with the two poems on love that
precede them.

Geoffrey Hartman writes of "Three years she grew"
that "The emphasis . . . is not on Lucy's death, but on the
consciousness of the survivor. It is something *unique*, and
the loss he feels includes the consciousness *that* it is
unique."[37] Hartman is right, I think. The elegiac tone of
"Three Years" is attributable less to the death of a girl of
uncertain age and relationship to the speaker than to "The
memory of what has been, / And never more will be." The
account of Lucy's fate is accomplished with two words

[36] Arthur Beatty, *William Wordsworth: His Doctrine and Art in
their Historical Relations* (3rd ed.; Madison: University of Wisconsin
Press, 1960), p. 213. David Ferry is right to say that in this poem "we
are made to feel two exactly contradictory feelings," pity for the
speaker and a sense that Lucy's death "is justified and right." *The
Limits of Mortality* (Middletown: Wesleyan University Press, 1959),
p. 76.

[37] Geoffrey H. Hartman, *Wordsworth's Poetry, 1787–1814* (New
Haven and London: Yale University Press, 1964), pp. 160–161.

("She died"). Wordsworth's main interest is in what she has bequeathed to her lover (or brother or father). She has left him a number of natural objects, unified into a scene, which once had a particular emotional significance and value, and have it no longer. Lucy and the Winander boy, both of them probable representatives of the child Wordsworth, are the occasions, not the subjects of the two poems. Despite the elegiac tone of both, neither implies that the adult, bereft of his own childhood impulses, has also been left a visible universe barren of meaning. But the tone is justified, as it is in the "Intimations Ode," because for a response gained there is a response lost. The childlike feeling of being "at home" in Nature that belonged to the Wordsworth who was the Winander boy, and perhaps the Lucy of "Three Years," will never come again. In short, perhaps Coleridge was only half right about the heroine of that poem. The morbid fear may have been Wordsworth's immediate response to the irrevocable loss of childhood, to which even the most intense memory and imagination can offer only a vicarious return.

There follow in the arrangement of 1815 five poems which would not have been placed among the "Poems of the Imagination," as Wordsworth explains in two notes, "but to avoid a needless multiplication of the Classes."[38] The first two of these, "The Horn of Egremont Castle" and "Goody Blake and Harry Gill," were later transferred to the "Miscellaneous Poems," because Wordsworth felt that "they rather refer to the imagination than are produced by it "[39] and his announced aim in the Preface was to group the poems of fancy and imagination according to the powers

[38] 1815 ed., I, 316.
[39] *Ibid.*

predominant in the production of them. Both poems, like *Peter Bell*, are psychological case studies which demonstrate the power of imagination to quicken in the minds of wicked men a terrifying fear of supernatural retribution. In the first, as in *Peter Bell*, the reader is in on the secret that the apparently supernatural event described is the natural result of the activity of imagination as it works upon the dormant conscience of the sinner. When the evil Hubert hears a blast of the horn "which none could sound, . . . / Save He who came as rightful Heir," his feverish imagination leads him to believe that the brother whose murder he had arranged has come to haunt him; feeling fear and remorse he confesses his sin and enters a religious sanctuary, where he dies. The reader is then assured in the final stanza that the attempted murder was frustrated and that Hubert's remorse was the result not of a supernatural event but of the moral power of imagination. The hero of the second of these poems, Harry Gill, is, like Peter Bell, a man whom constant experience with Nature has failed to soften. Like Peter, therefore, his sense of guilt must be produced by the power of imagination, working by means apparently supernatural. When Harry accosts the unfortunate Goody Blake, she invokes a curse that he will "never more be warm." Given this suggestion, Harry's imagination does the rest and his own guilty conscience, forced into action by a fear of the supernatural, convinces him that the curse has been fulfilled.

Of the third of the five poems that he hesitated to include in the class, "I wandered lonely as a cloud," Wordsworth writes that "The subject of these Stanzas is rather an elementary feeling and simple impression (approaching to the nature of an ocular spectrum) upon the imaginative faculty, than an *exertion* of it."[40] The sign for this footnote appears beside the line, "They flash upon that inward eye," and presumably identifies the faculty of imagination as this "inward eye." The meaning of this note, which has been ignored by critics, is extremely important as a comment on the symbolic mode of Wordsworth's poems of imagination and on the usual method by which such poems were composed. What Wordsworth means here is that the significance of the experience described was not the product of the time of the experience, for then he "gazed—and gazed—but little thought / What wealth the show to me had brought." This poem, therefore, is essentially different from those of this class discussed so far. In such poems as "There Was a Boy," "To the Cuckoo," and "A Night-Piece," symbols of eternity seem to have been inspired by the experiences themselves at the very time these experiences occurred, and in this sense these poems have as their subject *exertions* of the faculty of imagination and present descriptions of the very process by which it "half-creates" the world in which it operates. For this reason, we should be prepared to accept Wordsworth's distinction between such poems as these and the poem on the daffodils, for in the latter we find the imagination at a further remove from the experience; its subject is not the imagination in its act of transforming scene into symbol, but an overt comment on the effect of a recollected scene on a present feeling. In this poem it is not an emotion produced by an earlier co-operation of senses and imagination that Wordsworth recollects, but the scene itself, invested with profound feeling years after the original experience has passed.

Of the next two poems, "The Reverie of Poor Susan"

[40] *Ibid.*, I, 329.

and the "Power of Music," Wordsworth remarks that they
do not properly belong in the class of Imagination because
they are reveries, a statement important in its implied
distinction between visions of reality and imaginative
delusion.[41] That the moods described in the poems are
delusions Wordsworth makes quite clear. The song of a
bird transports Susan, in her mind, from the sordid reality
of urban life to a rural scene of her childhood. But the
moment passes; the transport is clearly illusion:

> She looks, and her heart is in heaven: but they fade,
> The mist and the river, the hill and the shade:
> The stream will not flow, and the hill will not rise,
> And the colours have all passed away from her eyes!

There is nothing here of the re-creating power of imagination. The physical scene is unyielding and, as we would
express it, Susan's daydream has played a trick on her. A
similar illusion is produced by the fiddler of the "Power of
Music," and, like Susan's "vision," it is possible only in a
trance-like state that can exist only for a short time. The
motley urban crowd is in effect hypnotized by the music,
but the stubborn reality of the scene is insisted upon and they
are blind to it only because they are "happy as souls in a
dream." It is more than coincidence that both these reveries
take place in a crowded city, for, with very few exceptions,
the power of Wordsworth's imagination to gain real
visions demanded a setting appropriate to the natural
sublime.

The next four poems were later shifted to the class called
"Memorials of a Tour in Scotland, 1803," but because of
their peculiarly imaginative symbolism they belong among

[41] *Ibid.*

the poems of imagination. Since the five poems just discussed constitute a hiatus in the scheme of Wordsworth's arrangement, it would be most faithful to Wordsworth's plan to consider these Scotch poems as immediately following those about Lucy, all eight poems of this group demonstrating the employment of the imagination "upon the feelings." The Scotch poems have in common the setting of solitude and calm so characteristic of Wordsworth's poems of vision, and they share as well the theme that man is afforded brief glimpses into "the life of things" by the stimulus of incidents apparently insignificant. Thus the simple greeting of the girl in "Stepping Westward" becomes more than a greeting; it is "The very sound of courtesy," evidence of the immanent spirit of love at work in the universe, not only in man or even in what are commonly called living creatures, but in all objects of Nature. Because this active principle pervades the universe, he can speak in the next poem, "Glen Almain," of "austere / Yet happy feelings of the dead," who are not dead in our usual sense of the term, since everything in Nature is alive. All the seemingly insignificant events related in these poems—the greeting in "Stepping Westward," the song of "The Solitary Reaper," and the encounter with the Highland girl—are alike evidences of the benign spirit of love in all of Nature. Because this is true, the poet carries from each incident one of those "spots of time" that remain to feed the imagination when the fleeting moments of vision have passed. In "To a Highland Girl" Wordsworth expresses this faith:

> Now thanks to Heaven! that of its grace
> Hath led me to this lonely place.
> Joy have I had; and going hence

I bear away my recompense.
In spots like these it is we prize
Our Memory, feel that she hath eyes:
Then, why should I be loth to stir?
I feel this place was made for her;
To give new pleasure like the past,
Continued long as life shall last.

The acknowledgment of the divine source of this grace is not a rhetorical flourish, but a basic tenet of Wordsworth's faith in imagination. The greeting in "Stepping Westward" also "seemed to be / A kind of *heavenly* destiny," for Wordsworth's poems of imagination are essentially religious verse, dedicated to the spirit of love that manifests itself to the imagination in everyday events; and such spots of time are evidence that this spirit resides in all things, and that these moments of vision can be found to be "A simple produce of the common day."[42]

His belief that the most simple incidents and objects can present to the imagination evidence of an "active universe" often led Wordsworth to value more highly than have his readers poems that owe their significance to an intuition afforded him by experiences which inspired these poems. Because these intuitions are personal and their deepest meaning beyond the power of words, the artistic success of his poetic expressions of them is not always equal to the value they had for him *as* experiences. This accounts for Wordsworth's tendency to prize too highly poems that lack great merit purely as poetry, and in evaluating his criticism we should take care to remember that to him poetry was primarily a moral concern and that he valued the imagination not only as the faculty which creates poetry but also—

[42] "Prospectus to *The Recluse*," l. 55.

and indeed chiefly—as the "inward eye" that affords man glimpses of truth which are "to the human eye / Invisible, yet liveth to the heart" (*Prelude*, II, 404–405). It is with this in mind that we should approach the next poem of this group, "Written in March," which ends in a tone wholly incongruous with its purely poetic claims:

> There's joy in the mountains;
> There's life in the fountains;
> Small clouds are sailing,
> Blue sky prevailing;
> The rain is over and gone!

Many readers would hesitate to honor a poem like this one by referring it to the imagination, but to deny it the title is to miss the point that as the record of a moment which revealed to Wordsworth the spirit in Nature, this poem is a production of that faculty which is solely responsible for visionary insight.

In his very brief delineation in the Preface of 1815 of the arrangement of "Poems of the Imagination," Wordsworth writes that "the Class is concluded with imaginative pictures of moral, political and religious sentiments."[43] Actually this account is descriptive more of his subsequent collected works than of the 1815 edition, for almost all the poems that he later added to this class deal with political and religious themes. In 1815 only one poem has a theme which might more accurately be called religious than moral and none, not even the poem on the French Revolution, is directly and explicitly concerned with politics. As I have interpreted the arrangement, the poem "Written in March" concludes the second major group within the class, concerned with the

43 *PW*, II, 440.

employment of imagination upon "feelings, characters, and actions." Beginning with "Gipsies" the subject is that of his third group, the exertions of the imagination upon moral sentiments. The group's major theme follows logically in the overall design of Wordsworth's arrangement of the poems of this class, which is to trace the growth of the imagination. The first group deals with the earliest impressions and influences on that faculty of "various objects of the external universe," the second, with the application of the power of imagination to typical human situations, characteristics, and action. The next group is designed to illustrate the manner in which the imagination functions as a discoverer of moral truths. These poems differ from those of the second group, which also concern essentially human feelings, in that they attempt to extract explicit moral statements from the situations and actions which they describe.

"Gipsies," the first of these poems, has often been emphatically censured, beginning with Coleridge, who cited it as an example of "*mental* bombast," a disparity between matter and manner.[44] Presumably Coleridge's criticism was responsible for the radical revision that Wordsworth made in the conclusion of the poem. In the early version his attitude toward the idleness of the gipsies is unequivocal:

> Behold the mighty Moon! this way
> She looks as if at them—but they
> Regard not her:—oh better wrong and strife
> Better vain deeds or evil than such life!
> The silent Heavens have goings-on;
> The stars have tasks—but these have none.

[44] *BL*, II, 109.

The boldness of this exclamation is still present in the final version, but carefully qualified:

> Behold the mighty Moon! this way
> She looks as if at them—but they
> Regard not her:—oh better wrong and strife
> (By nature transient) than this torpid life;
> Life which the very stars reprove
> As on their silent tasks they move!
> Yet, witness all that stirs in heaven or earth!
> In scorn I speak not;—they are what their birth
> And breeding suffer them to be;
> Wild outcasts of society!

The thundering denunciation of 1807 has been softened to a rather condescending sociological explanation. Wordsworth later came to regret this alteration and to feel that "the concluding apology should be cancelled";[45] he was right to feel so, because Coleridge's criticism of this poem and, for that matter, of Wordsworth's "mental bombast" in general, reflects his misunderstanding of Wordsworth's use in poetry of apparently trivial incidents. The theme of "Gipsies" is perhaps best defined by Helen Darbishire: "the sublime poetic expression of a mood in which the poet, active in mind and body, feeling himself consciously at one with the activities of the universe, is impressed by the spectacle of stagnant life, so picturesquely presented to his imagination by the gipsies."[46] The gipsies are subjected to the poet's indignation because their closeness to Nature and isolation from the distractions of a busy civilization afford them ideal opportunities to receive the impulses that were to Wordsworth evidence of a spirit of love in the universe.

[45] Quoted in *PW*, II, 509.
[46] Quoted in *PW*, II, 509.

For this reason, their idleness is more than lack of industry: it is the mark of their indifference to the sources of sublimity that were the foundation of his faith. His condemnation is not a utilitarian demand for ambition and productivity, but a cry of outrage that even men in a favored position fail to take advantage of Nature's power to nourish the soul. They are wrong because they do not "regard" the moon, just as Peter Bell is wrong to see no significance in a primrose by a river's brim.[47]

"Gipsies" is followed by a companion piece, "Beggars." In the former poem Wordsworth maintains that even evil action is preferable to the indifference and sloth of the gipsies ("Better vain deeds or evil than such life"). In "Beggars" lies the proof that this cry is not mere rhetoric, for it is precisely an evil (or, at least, sinful) deed that is the poem's subject; yet for Wordsworth this deed is a source of joy, not sorrow. The story of the poem is deceptively simple. The speaker is accosted by a beggar woman who grossly exaggerates the sorrow of her condition: ". . . on our English land / Such woes, I knew, could never be." He responds, nevertheless, to her plea for charity. After leaving the woman he meets two young boys, obviously her sons; and when they too plead for alms, he tells them of his encounter with their mother. Their response carries the theme of the poem. Twice they lie, insisting that their mother has long been dead. And when he challenges this statement: ". . . in the twinkling of an eye, / 'Come! come!'

[47] In 1827 "Ruth," formerly included among the "Poems Founded on the Affections," was shifted to the "Poems of the Imagination," and in its final position it immediately follows "Gipsies." This was an appropriate alteration because, like the gipsies, Ruth's lover lived in solitude among the great forces of Nature, but failed to profit from his favored situation.

cried one, and without more ado / Off to some other play the joyous Vagrants flew!" In bare outline there is little in the poem to suggest why Wordsworth, fifteen years later, composed a sequel to it, which ends with this passionate tribute to the young boys:

> Kind Spirits! may we not believe
> That they, so happy and so fair
> Through your sweet influence, and the care
> Of pitying Heaven, at least were free
> From touch of *deadly* injury?
> Destined, whate'er their earthly doom,
> For mercy and immortal bloom?

In 1827 Wordsworth added to "Beggars" a stanza that makes quite clear his attitude toward the children, by contrasting them to their mother:

> Yet *they*, so blithe of heart, seemed fit
> For finest tasks of earth or air:
> Wings let them have, and they might flit
> Precursors to Aurora's car,
> Scattering fresh flowers; though happier far, I ween,
> To hunt their fluttering game o'er rock and level green.

The lying of the boys is a performance that they have been ordered to enact, but so little is it a part of their real nature that they perform it perfunctorily and readily fly off "to some *other* play," for play it is to them. Their natural goodness and joy are the qualities Wordsworth dwells on, and these are gifts that result from their harmony with the fresh and vital impulses of Nature. They are neither idle and indifferent to Nature, as are the gypsies, nor bowed by the sorrows of adult life, as is their mother; for them "the daedal earth / Was filled with animated toys, / And implements of frolic mirth" ("Sequel to the Foregoing," ll. 2–4).

Wordsworth's purpose in these poems on the gypsies and the beggars is to show how Nature's message of joy lies all about us but must be received by minds in tune with the active spirit of the universe. This theme led him to commemorate his chance meeting with the boys in the sequel to "Beggars":

> They met me in a genial hour,
> When universal nature breathed
> As with the breath of one sweet flower,—
> A time to overrule the power
> Of discontent, and check the birth
> Of thoughts with better thoughts at strife,
> The most familiar bane of life
> Since parting Innocence bequeathed
> Mortality to Earth!

When we recall that to both Wordsworth and Coleridge the word *genial* meant the power to feel imaginatively and that this power is the gift solely of the unconscious joy that harmony with Nature makes possible, we recognize here a familiar theme, the correction of despondency by a return to the springs of life that are the natural bounty of youth.

The next four poems in this third group are further explorations of the ways by which an adult can regain the sense of intimacy with life's vital forces that was his without effort in childhood and youth. The two Yarrow poems are illustrations of the process by which the imagination invests sense data with a meaning that sense alone cannot offer. In the first, "Yarrow Unvisited," Wordsworth confesses a fear that to subject his imaginative vision of the stream to the senses would be "To have a soulless image on the eye /

That had usurped upon a living thought" (*Prelude*, VI, 526–527). To the senses, especially the senses of an adult, the scene would be devoid of wonder, and in the following lines Wordsworth pictures it as the mere senses would:

> "What's Yarrow but a river bare,
> That glides the dark hills under?
> There are a thousand such elsewhere
> As worthy of your wonder."

Better, then, not to risk the vision that the imagination has made possible:

> "Be Yarrow stream unseen, unknown!
> It must, or we shall rue it:
> We have a vision of our own;
> Ah! why should we undo it?
> The treasured dreams of times long past,
> We'll keep them, winsome Marrow!
> For when we're there, although 'tis fair,
> 'Twill be another Yarrow!"

This fear is justified, and Wordsworth picks up the same theme in the opening lines of "Yarrow Visited":

> And is this—Yarrow?—*This* the Stream
> Of which my fancy cherished,
> So faithfully, a waking dream?
> An image that hath perished!
> O that some Minstrel's harp were near,
> To utter notes of gladness,
> And chase this silence from the air,
> That fills my heart with sadness!

Wordsworth next asks himself *why* this sadness should be, since the scene that the senses present is itself quite beautiful, and indeed "Dost rival in the light of day" the "delicate creation" of "fond imagination." But he had already answered this question in the first Yarrow poem: "For when we're there, although 'tis fair, / 'Twill be *another* Yarrow!" Everything that the senses report is beautiful, but the scene can regain its significance to the soul only when the senses yield to the imagination:

> I see—but not by sight alone,
> Loved Yarrow, have I won thee;
> A ray of fancy still survives—
> Her sunshine plays upon thee!

Only when there is thrown over the scene "a certain colouring of imagination" (or here, rather curiously, of fancy) can it be cherished as a reinvigorating spot of time. It is because "A ray of fancy still survives" that Wordsworth can now be assured the scene will assume for him a significance that will last long after the visible scene has gone from his mind:

> The vapours linger round the Heights,
> They melt, and soon must vanish;
> One hour is theirs, nor more is mine—
> Sad thought, which I would banish,
> But that I know, where'er I go,
> Thy genuine image, Yarrow!
> Will dwell with me—to heighten joy,
> And cheer my mind in sorrow.

And this genuine image that outlives the sense impression is the product of imagination.

The next poem, "Star-Gazers," is another comment on the threat which the tyranny of the senses holds for imaginative vision. The people who eagerly wait to gaze into the heavens pass away after their glimpses through the telescope and "Seem to meet with little gain, seem less happy than before." Attempting to account for their apparent dissatisfaction, Wordsworth proposes several explanations, but the real answer, only implied in the poem, is that we cannot hope to gain ultimate meaning from a sense impression no matter how we "pry and pore." The most important values of the invisible world do not exist for the senses, and are not, therefore, within the province of mechanical aids to the sense. It is not by strengthening the hold of the senses on the scene that we shall obtain a "genuine image"; rather we must relinquish this hold altogether to the power of imagination, which alone can *create* meaning.[48]

This transforming power of imagination makes the poet's encounter with the leech-gatherer of "Resolution and Independence" a profoundly meaningful experience. It is not the senses alone but the poet's imagination as well that thus paints the scene of their meeting:

> All things that love the sun are out of doors;
> The sky rejoices in the morning's birth;
> The grass is bright with rain-drops;—on the moors
> The hare is running races in her mirth;
> And with her feet she from the plashy earth
> Raises a mist; that, glittering in the sun,
> Runs with her all the way, wherever she doth run.

[48] Cf. the following lines from MS. Y of *The Prelude* (p. 575):

> As his powers advance,
> He is not like a man who sees in the heavens
> A blue vault merely and a glittering cloud,
>
> . . . .
> Without the glass of Galileo sees
> What Galileo saw; and as it were

The effect of the scene depends principally upon an imaginative intuition of the joyful harmony of all Nature, an intuition of which sense impression is but the foundation. The speaker's senses tell him only that the sky is cloudless; imagination, that it "rejoices." Similarly it is not the words of the leech-gatherer that correct despondency, but the transformation of the scene and the old man which is wrought by imagination. The old man's voice is "like a stream / Scarce heard," and his body vanishes into a dream-like vision, until he becomes a creature of imagination: "like a man from some far region sent, / To give me human strength, by apt admonishment." During the time that the imagination is creating meaning from sense experience, the leech-gatherer himself is never really what he is to the eye, but a thing of imagination, of the "mind's eye"; and this is the reason for the poet's dazed state and the repeated question, "How is it that you live, and what is it you do?", so often ridiculed by Wordsworth's critics. At the conclusion of the poem when the speaker tells us that to cheer his mind in later periods of dejection he will "think of the Leech-gatherer on the lonely moor," he is speaking not of the old man of his sense perception, but of the image of "human strength" that the imagination has created out of the data of sense. The poem begins with the picture of calm after a storm, and it ends in the same way. The assurance of recovery inherent in the natural cycle becomes in the course of the narrative the basis for the poet's own mental progress from agitation to tranquillity. The old leech-gatherer, to whom Wordsworth gives attributes of both

---

Resolving into one great faculty
Of being bodily eye and spiritual need,
The converse which he holds is limitless.   (ll. 139–155)

man and Nature, provides the symbolic link between the two. The leech-gatherer might be compared to the emblems of poems of fancy, but the comparison could be made only as an intellectual exercise. The difference between the picture in this poem and that, say, of "The Oak and the Broom" is more easily experienced than explained, but the explanation would go something like this: the Oak stands for Pride, and these are two terms of an allegory. The leech-gatherer does not stand for resolution and independence, and, Wordsworth's title to the contrary, cannot be comfortably contained in any allegorical label: he *is* resolution and independence, just as Lucy Gray is "The Spirit of Solitude." He belongs not to allegory, but to myth, and myth for Wordsworth is a means of giving form to a feeling without form. In myth, feeling and image are one and the image is, in Coleridge's words, a "translucence of the eternal through and in the temporal," at once accessible to earthly senses and transcending them.[49]

The next three poems in this group have in common the theme of how imagination at times invests objects and incidents with moral significance by appealing to superstition, a primitive but powerful agent of morality. The note to the first of the three, "The Thorn," describes the superstitious man as one who has "a reasonable share of imagination, ... the faculty which produces impressive effects out of simple elements,"[50] and though the incidents in the third poem, "Song at the Feast of Brougham Castle," cannot be called simple, in all three poems the events described derive much of their significance from the

[49] *The Complete Works of Samuel Taylor Coleridge*, ed. W. G. T. Shedd (New York: Harper and Brothers, 1868–1871), I, 437.
[50] *PW*, II, 512.

superstitious imaginings of the simple people whom we are to envision as the narrators of these stories. Thus the thorn, despite the matter-of-fact description of the old seaman ("I've measured it from side to side; / 'Tis three feet long, and two feet wide"), has the power to arouse awe and horror in the minds of the narrator's simple neighbors. Wordsworth's own account of the origin of the poem explains that he hoped to produce a similar effect on his more sophisticated audience:

> [The poem] Arose out of my observing, on the ridge of Quantock Hill, on a stormy day, a thorn which I had often passed in calm and bright weather without noticing it. I said to myself, "Cannot I by some invention do as much to make this Thorn permanently an impressive object as the storm has made it to my eyes at this moment?"[51]

Wordsworth's poem is "A power like one of Nature's" (*Prelude*, XIII, 312), providing for the reader of "The Thorn" the same incitement of the passions as the storm provided for Wordsworth. Both the natural and the poetic creation cast over a simple object a certain coloring of imagination, so that we not only observe the old seaman's association of ideas in a state of excitement, but duplicate this process in our own minds. The thorn is memorable for us for the same reason that it exerts such power over the narrator's imagination: it partakes of some ultimately unknowable higher reality, glimpsed variously by the superstitious and the sophisticated.

The moral value of this elevation of the superstitious mind may not be obvious, but we should remember that in Wordsworth's view stimulation of the imaginative powers

[51] *PW*, II, 511.

was an end in itself since by this process the sensibilities are activated and the sympathies expanded. In "The world is too much with us" his exclamation, "I'd rather be / A Pagan suckled in a creed outworn," is not mere rhetoric, but a primary theme in Book IV of *The Excursion*, which seeks to prove that "Superstition [is] better than apathy" and can serve as a means to correct despondency.[52]

The next poem, "Hart-Leap Well," also invokes superstitious legend in its inculcation of a moral, expounded in the last stanza of Part II:

"One lesson, Shepherd, let us two divide,
　Taught both by what she [Nature] shows, and what conceals;
　Never to blend our pleasure or our pride
　With sorrow of the meanest thing that feels."

The poem is divided into two parts, narrative and epilogue. The legend is narrated by a superstitious old shepherd to the more sophisticated poet, so that the meaning of the action is presented from their two points of view. To explain the decaying ruins of the pleasure-house built by the knight to commemorate his successful chase of a hart, the old man assumes that "the spot is curst" because of the death of "that unhappy Hart." To the poet it does not matter that the shepherd's view is superstitious so long as he extracts the correct moral from the events described; and he can honestly say to the old man, "Small difference lies between thy creed and mine," for the truth they have perceived by different means is the same truth:

　　This Beast not unobserved by Nature fell;
　　His death was mourned by sympathy divine.

52 From the Argument to Book IV, "Despondency Corrected."

Whatever the source of this belief, the important thing is the belief itself: there is an active spirit of love in the universe that extends to all creatures. This spirit makes known its presence in a variety of ways, and Wordsworth sought to show in his poetry that to him at least it did not disdain to speak through the simple objects and events of Nature, that, indeed, the scenes of everyday experience are the favorite milieu of these divine communications.

The next poem, "Yes, it was the mountain Echo," in one way is notably different from the others of this group. In the preceding poems of imagination, Wordsworth's intimations of the spirit in Nature, the common subject of all these poems, are not presented in the terminology of orthodox Christianity, and it is worth noting that in his final arrangement for the edition of 1849–1850, the position of this poem is altered so that it now stands as the last of all but one of those poems included in the "Poems of the Imagination" in the 1815 edition. In its new position it serves to introduce the poems that Wordsworth later added to this class, almost all of which are more direct in expression of a moral and more overtly Christian in terminology. In "Yes, it was the mountain Echo" there are distinct overtones of orthodox Christian doctrine, one of which, the sharp distinction between man's divine and carnal natures, appears in the third stanza. Drawing a comparison between the purely natural cry of the cuckoo and its echo, which is "Like her ordinary cry, / Like—but oh, how different!", Wordsworth then derives a moral analogy:

> Hears not also mortal Life?
> Hear not we, unthinking Creatures!
> Slaves of folly, love, or strife—
> Voices of two different natures?

The particular character of Wordsworth's religion, as contradistinguished from what has been called his animism or pantheism, is not my concern here, except as his unquestioned later emphasis on orthodox faith affected the themes and modes of his later poems of imagination and fancy. What is certainly beyond question is that after about 1806 he ceased to rely on imaginative re-creations of visionary experiences and turned to rational statement of moral lessons. In the words of Basil Willey, "Wordsworth to some extent abandoned Nature ... abandoned it first for 'Duty,' and then for Faith." And as a result "Much of his later poetry deals with experiences and subjects other than the moments of vision which are admittedly his special prerogative. ..."[53]

One popular explanation for Wordsworth's retreat from faith in experience to faith in orthodox creeds is the subject of the next poem, the "French Revolution" (lines later incorporated in *The Prelude*, XI, 105–144), which was first published as a separate poem in Coleridge's journal, *The Friend*, in 1809. The bitter effects of Wordsworth's disappointment over the course of events after the French Revolution are well known. The most important of these effects, from our point of view, is that in his projected great work, *The Recluse*, the central theme was to be the power of Nature to correct the despondencies arising from man's loss of faith in his purely rational faculties. This is also the unifying theme of all the poems of imagination (and, to a lesser extent, poems of fancy) composed before 1806. After this year, so far as his poetry records, Nature herself could no longer serve his purpose; he turned instead to more

[53] Basil Willey, *The Eighteenth Century Background* (London: Chatto and Windus, 1949), p. 292.

traditional and orthodox sources of comfort, particularly to those tenets of Christian faith that recommend the stoic virtues of duty, meekness, and forbearance.

Whether or not Wordsworth was aware of it when he composed the lines on the Revolution, the poem contains hints that, in retrospect, to some extent prepare us for his loss of faith in moments of vision; for in this poem it is not primarily to rational powers that his misplaced faith in the Revolution is ascribed. It is not the understanding that first prepared men to be duped by this event, but rather communion with Nature herself:

> They who had fed their childhood upon dreams,
> The playfellows of fancy, who had made
> All powers of swiftness, subtilty, and strength
> Their ministers,—who in lordly wise had stirred
> Among the grandest objects of the sense,
> And dealt with whatsoever they found there
> As if they had within some lurking right
> To wield it;—they, too, who, of gentle mood
> Had watched all gentle motions, and to these
> Had fitted their own thoughts . . . .

In Book IX of *The Prelude*, reflecting on his early response to the Revolution, Wordsworth remarks that he was emotionally in sympathy with the stated aims and principles of the revolutionists because his own experience, his own instruction from Nature, made these events seem "nothing out of nature's certain course" (l. 247). He had, he says, felt

> subservience from the first
> To presences of God's mysterious power
> Made manifest in Nature's sovereignty,
>
> .   .   .   .

> To sanction the proud workings of the soul,
> And mountain liberty.   (ll. 233–238)

But if Nature's training could result in such delusion as that of his faith in the Revolution, might one not come eventually to doubt Nature's lessons, or—more probably this was Wordsworth's fate—to doubt man's ability to read aright these lessons? A dramatic illustration of this change in orientation from Nature to God and from visionary experience to orthodox Christian derivation of moral is provided by the final arrangement of the "Poems of the Imagination," where the "French Revolution," which ends with an expression of hope that man will find his happiness "in the very world, which is the world / Of all of us," is followed by the poem on the "Mountain Echo," which ends with this stanza:

> Such rebounds our inward ear
> Catches sometimes from afar—
> Listen, ponder, hold them dear;
> For of God,—of God they are.

In the 1815 edition, on the other hand, the poem on the French Revolution was followed by one that sounds a similar note of optimism and faith in man's powers. In "It is no Spirit who from heaven hath flown," the spectacle of Hesperus, that "most ambitious Star," does not instill in the poet the idea that men are "Slaves of folly, love, or strife," but instead provides an image for human aspiration. It suggests to him not the need for meekness and humility, but

> That I might step beyond my natural race
> As thou seem'st now to do; might one day trace
> Some ground not mine; and, strong her strength above,

135

My Soul, an Apparition in the place,
Tread there with steps that no one shall reprove!

Increasingly, Wordsworth came to attribute less power to man and more to some spirit from above, descending to offer guidance and admonition.

According to Wordsworth's letter of 1809, the large group of poems which included those classified in 1815 as "Poems of the Fancy" and "Poems of the Imagination" was to be concluded by "Tintern Abbey." In later editions, however, this poem is far from the last of the poems of imagination. The significance of this change can hardly be overestimated, for "Tintern Abbey" is regarded by almost all Wordsworthian scholars as one of the most unequivocal utterances of his religion of Nature. Concerning the exact character of this faith there is much disagreement, but no amount of argument can obscure the fact that the transition from Wordsworth's characterization of himself in "Tintern Abbey" as "A worshipper of Nature" to the traditional Christian language of *The Excursion* reflects a major change. We have Wordsworth's word that he valued only religious poetry, and, by his own definition of such poetry, there is no doubt that he can properly be called a religious poet.[54] Because this is true, in his later years he could not allow "Tintern Abbey" to stand as his final expression in a class of poems that was to be "concluded with imaginative pictures of moral, political and religious sentiments." To have done so would have been to permit his readers to think that this poem represented most fully his mature religious faith.

This being the case, we might at first wonder why the poem was placed last even in the 1815 edition, for certainly

[54] See *LY*, I, 134–135.

long before then Wordsworth's faith and his religious language had become more orthodox; *The Excursion* had appeared the year before. One can surmise that even in 1815 the position of "Tintern Abbey" was tenuous. The reference in the Preface to the group's concluding with poems on political and religious sentiments was not an accurate description of the order of the class of Imagination in that edition. No poem of imagination, not even the "French Revolution," can properly be said to be concerned principally with political themes, and, except for "Tintern Abbey" itself, only the poem on the mountain echo is religious in the sense that Wordsworth would have meant in 1815. In describing the poems of this class Wordsworth was looking ahead to later collected editions, when he would include poems dealing directly with political and religious subjects. Most of the poems added to the class after 1815 did not exist at that time and the few that did were assigned to other classes. With the addition of these later poems he was able to conclude the class as he had promised. The language and sentiments of these poems were of the sort to appeal comfortably to his readers: they extolled the same virtues and castigated the same vices, both political and religious, that the orthodox English reader had been taught to praise and to deplore.

Much as the modern reader may regret that the concluding poems of the class of imagination are products not of Wordsworth's Nature philosophy and the Great Decade, but of the period of religious and aesthetic orthodoxy, he cannot fail to see that this plan is true to the basic principle that guided the arrangement of 1809 and, less obviously, that of 1815: that the poems be arranged "according to an order of time, commencing with Childhood, and terminating with

Old Age, Death, and Immortality." To this principle the final arrangement remains faithful, for it does indeed trace the growth of Wordsworth's mind, from his youthful trust in direct and untranslatable experiences of the spirit of Nature to a later dependence on the traditional lessons of his "moral Muse." It is therefore quite appropriate that the class of poems which begins with an image of a boy receiving into his very being "the visible scene" of Nature should conclude with distinct echoes of familiar scripture:

A Voice to Light gave Being;
To Time, and Man his earth-born chronicler;

.   .   .   .

.   .   .   .   though earth be dust
And vanish, though the heavens dissolve, her [Harmony's] stay
Is in the WORD, that shall not pass away.[55]

[55] "On the Power of Sound," ll. 209–210, 222–224.

6

Imagination and the Sublime

Modern scholarship has all but buried the old notion that
the Romantic poets were careless songbirds, indifferent to
the craft of poetry, if not actually scornful of it. We have
learned how to read those glittering aphorisms about poetry
that once seemed so definitive—such as Shelley's "when
composition begins, inspiration is already on the decline,"
or Keats' "if Poetry comes not as naturally as the Leaves to
a tree it had better not come at all."[1] We have learned to
qualify Wordsworth's memorable words on the origin of
poetry, "the spontaneous overflow of powerful feelings,"
as he himself qualified them: "and though this be true,
Poems to which any value can be attached were never
produced on any variety of subjects but by a man who,
being possessed of more than usual organic sensibility, had
also thought long and deeply."[2] Yet this myth about the
Romantic view of poetry is like most myths: it veils an
important truth. No group of English poets made bolder

[1] From "A Defence of Poetry," *The Complete Works of Percy
Bysshe Shelley*, ed. Roger Ingpen and Walter E. Peck (Julian Edition;
London: Ernest Benn Ltd., 1927–1930), VII, 135; Keats to John
Taylor, February 27, 1818. *The Letters of John Keats*, ed. Hyder E.
Rollins (Cambridge: Harvard University Press, 1958), I, 238–239.

[2] *PW*, II, 387–388.

and higher claims for poetry, but none more consistently regarded poetry as a means toward the attainment of some end that is more religious than aesthetic.

The faith that distinguishes Romantic poets from all others was not a faith in poetry itself. Poetry was their means, and so many of their poems are poems about poetry because means can be questioned when the end must not be. Their faith was really in imagination, specifically in the imaginative vision that precedes composition, and in their terms a poet is first of all a man capable of visionary experience and only secondarily a writer of verse. Poetry was important to them principally because it seemed to be the best hope of transmuting vision into expression; it was important because "Poesy alone can tell her dreams," and tell them in such a way that vision undergoes the least possible loss in the process. This was the assumption of all the major Romantic poets—with the possible exception of Byron, in whom the aristocratic disdain for the Romantic divinization of the poet may have gone deeper than pose. As recent scholars of romanticism have repeatedly explained, the joyful affirmations of the Romantic poets were at least in part attempts to exorcise their fears that the ground of their faith was slipping from beneath them. Poetry and religion, repeatedly linked by these poets, faced a common fate in a world that was rushing toward a final severence between the world of eye and ear and some transcendent other world.

The final outcome of this process has yet to be decided, but so far it has forced those modern poets who inherited the Romantic emphasis on imagination to divert their visions and energies to the world as defined by science and common sense. The result is the substitution of poetry itself as a sublimation for the imaginative faith that once looked through poetry to the transcendent reality that gave Romantic poetry its sense of mission. With the metaphysical grounds of poetry no longer available, there remains only the poem itself with its tragically defiant declaration of independence from logic belonging to the world that all of us, even poets, acknowledge against our wills to be the real world. In Wordsworth we can witness Romantic faith at its strongest, and in his failure to maintain that faith is implied the failure of romanticism to resist the terrible fear that poetry is an escape from reality, not a way into it, a delusion nobler than that supplied by "Bacchus and his pards" but ultimately no more enduring. We may disagree over whether Keats intended the pun, but whichever the case, in speaking of "the *viewless* wings of Poesy," he raised the questions to which romanticism provides no completely reassuring answers: "Was it a vision, or a waking dream? / Fled is that music:—Do I wake or sleep?" Wordsworth never put these questions so baldly, and for a time he could write with an apparent assurance that poetry, like religion, is "ethereal and transcendent."[3]

Wordsworth has often been called the most English of poets. So he is in many ways, and he is perhaps most English in simultaneously scorning and making use of metaphysical speculations. On his scale of values, forms and categories trailed far behind sensation and experience; intuition or instinct was far more trustworthy than any abstractions that the understanding employs to domesticate reality. The two chief monuments commemorating his painful efforts to meet Coleridge's demand for a truly

[3] *PW*, II, 412.

141

philosophic poem are the disappointing *Excursion* and the incomplete *Recluse*; reaching for metaphysical heights, he could only fall back on the platitudes of his youth. Nevertheless, he firmly believed that poetry can be a path to truths hidden from most men, and he lived in an age of exciting new speculations about the power of imagination. His famous lines on the French Revolution—"Bliss was it in that dawn to be alive, / But to be young was very Heaven!"—might be applied equally well to a quieter upheaval whose influence was beginning to reach nineteenth-century England, Immanuel Kant's "Copernican Revolution of the Mind." The political event has received more than its due as a force in English romanticism, but the intellectual revolution was more lastingly congenial to Romantic poetry and aesthetics.

Today, many years after the pioneer studies of scholars like Shawcross and Bradley, the fruitful confluence of German philosophy and English Romantic poetry is securely established as a subject of great importance in approaches to romanticism.[4] Whether or not one believes that Wordsworth was aware of the mutual interests of Romantic theories of imagination and the writings of Kant and his disciples, there is much to be gained by placing side by side these two great contributions to English thought in the first half of the nineteenth century. The similarities between Wordsworth's theory of imagination and the tenets of German idealism are partially hidden behind a vocabulary borrowed from English empiricism. He lacked Coleridge's

[4] See Professor Shawcross' masterful account of Coleridge's debt to Germany in his Introduction to the *Biographia Literaria*, *BL*, I, xi–lxxxix; and A. C. Bradley, "English Poetry and German Philosophy in the Age of Wordsworth," in *A Miscellany* (London: Macmillan and Co. Ltd., 1929), pp. 105–138.

knowledge of Kantian terminology and boasted of his ignorance. His modes of thought, however, found the vocabulary of empiricism too confining, and, apparently without realizing that he was doing so, he often expressed himself in a language and tone more reminiscent of Schelling, say, than of David Hartley. Such expressions are particularly evident in his comments on the sublime. Yet both he and Coleridge seem to have needed to trace their beliefs ultimately to a native source, and since the sublime had been given a decidedly English caste in the eighteenth century, they found this topic warmly familiar and natural.

Wordsworth's known remarks about the German Romantic philosophers are smugly derogatory, but his friend Crabb Robinson, who admired them, recognized in Wordsworth a kindred spirit. According to Robinson, Wordsworth "represented . . . much as, unknown to him, the German philosophers have done—that by the imagination the mere fact is exhibited as connected with that infinity without which there is no poetry."⁵ Robinson was simply jotting down an impression, and a word like *connected* conveys little enough meaning. But in identifying the conjunction of mere fact and infinity as a key to Wordsworth's poetry, he gives some evidence that he was aware of the importance to Romantic theories of imagination of the alliance between sense perceptions of external reality and the deep truths to be discovered in and through these perceptions. In fact, Robinson's comment may remind us of Coleridge's description of a symbol as "the translucence of the eternal through and in the temporal," or of this observation by a twentieth-century American poet:

⁵ *Henry Crabb Robinson on Books and their Writers*, ed. Edith J. Morley (London: J. M. Dent and Sons Ltd., 1938), I, 191.

"—poetry exists only by a continuing revelation in a world always incarnate of word and flesh indissolubly, a world simultaneously solid and transpicuous."[6]

Object, perception, and imagination are three of the constituents of Wordsworth's visionary experiences. The fourth is the set of conditions under which the other three come together most fruitfully. Most of Wordsworth's speculations about this fourth element can profitably be arranged under the rubric, the sublime.[7] For Wordsworth the sublime is not a quality to be found in certain objects, or even a quality inherent in the mind. It is rather the grounds for visionary experience. His conception of the sublime is at the root of his distinction between fancy and imagination and between the two kinds of poems produced by these faculties. No given object and subject can guarantee a visionary experience, for vision is the result of the whole complex of relationships that constitutes experience of objects. The poet's duty is to prepare his imagination for vision by establishing "habits of meditation" that prompt and regulate his feelings and thereby increase his receptivity to these visions that come when they come, that cannot be induced; these habits of meditation are Wordsworth's

[6] *The Complete Works of Samuel Taylor Coleridge*, ed. W. G. T. Shedd (New York: Harper and Brothers, 1868–1871), I, 437; Howard Nemerov, "The Swaying Form: A Problem in Poetry," in *Poetry and Fiction: Essays* (New Brunswick: Rutgers University Press, 1963), p. 13.

[7] My chief debt in this chapter is to Samuel H. Monk's *The Sublime: A Study of Critical Theories in XVIII-Century England* (New York: Modern Language Association of America, 1935). Professor Monk's treatment of Wordsworth is brief but rich in implications, and even where my conclusions differ from his I am aware that I am building on the solid foundation of his scholarship. I also owe a great deal to Clarence D. Thorpe's "Coleridge on the Sublime," in *Wordsworth and*

spiritual exercises.[8] Precisely these habits distinguish poets from other men, and since habits are formed and maintained by exercise, the exertion required to compose a poem of imagination is itself an experience of ultimate reality. Whether writing a poem or living the experience that inspires it, the truly imaginative man knows that his habit of turning "from the treasures of time" to "those of eternity" is "presumptive evidence of a future state of existence."[9] It is no wonder that the Romantics extended the term *poet* to include any man of intense imagination.

One of the ironies of the Romantic period is the repeated insistence by its major figures that the poet must be a man speaking to men. Because this was so integral a part of their faith in poetry, which is to say their faith in imagination, readers' neglect and reviewers' charges of obscurity hurt them cruelly. No group of poets has expected more from readers, for they insisted that the success of poetry depends almost as much on the reader's imagination as on the poet's. This belief accounts for Coleridge's gratitude to German transcendental idealism and its fundamental tenet that imagination operates in every man as a faculty for organizing and unifying the discrete reports of the senses. Without the presence of such a faculty in readers of poetry, the poet would be an isolated genius, trapped by his own imaginative power in a world of experience whose meaning he could not share. Modern critics would probably say that something like this has happened to poets. Wordsworth was aware of

Coleridge: Studies in honor of George McLean Harper, ed. Earl Leslie Griggs (Princeton: Princeton University Press, 1939), pp. 192–219.

[8] On Wordsworth's "habits of meditation," see *PW*, II, 387, 395–396.

[9] *PW*, II, 412.

the danger, and his solution, a tragic one, was to make fewer demands on his readers.

While his faith was yet alive, he saw in man's response to the sublime the meeting ground of poet and reader. And so, in large measure, his faith in the efficacy of poetry was his faith in the sublime and in man's ability to experience it. In a sense, therefore, imagination and the sublime constitute one topic in Wordsworthian criticism, and one can endorse even today Clarence D. Thorpe's opinion that "Wordsworth's ideas on the sublime are worthy of more extended study than they have yet received." [10]

Samuel H. Monk likens the sublime to "a very full treasure box in which can be found all the paraphernalia of romantic writers."[11] There is no doubt that the rediscovery of the treatise attributed to Longinus is a major landmark in any study of what we call pre-romanticism. But like the

[10] Thorpe, "Coleridge on the Sublime," *Wordsworth and Coleridge*, p. 207 n. In 1806 Wordsworth wrote to Lady Beaumont, "I have received a very obliging letter from Mr. Price, who seems much pleased with what I said upon the sublime." Since Uvedale Price was the author of *Essay on the Picturesque*, we might assume that Wordsworth would have been careful to give a rather full account of his thinking on the sublime. It is particularly unfortunate, therefore, that his communication to Price has not been found. See *MY*, I, 30. After I had written this chapter, Professor John Nabholtz, now at the University of Rochester, called to my attention a long fragment of an essay by Wordsworth on the sublime and the beautiful. The original of this fragment, included among a manuscript of the *Guide to the Lakes*, is in the Dove Cottage Library at Grasmere (Prose MS. 28) and a copy is in the Wordsworth Collection at Cornell. The essay will be published for the first time in the forthcoming Oxford edition of Wordsworth's prose being prepared by Professor W. J. B. Owen of University College of North Wales and Professor Jane Worthington Smyser of Connecticut College.

[11] Monk, *The Sublime*, pp. 140–141.

term *romanticism* itself, *the sublime* meant various things to various writers. In its simplest sense, it came to be used in the eighteenth century to exalt the spontaneous and irregular in art and Nature at the expense of the more polished and artful. If this were Wordsworth's concept of the term, its usefulness for us would be negligible; for if Pope could invoke it to praise Homer over Virgil, and Dryden to defend the irregularities of Shakespeare from stricture according to the rules of dramatic composition, it would not go far toward illuminating Wordsworth's doctrine of imagination. Fortunately we have Wordsworth's assurance that his notion of the sublime was not the popular one: "One is surprized that it should have been supposed for a moment, that *Longinus* writes upon the Sublime, even in our vague and popular sense of the word—What is there in Sappho's ode that has any affinity with the sublimity of Ezekiel or Isaiah, or even of Homer or Eschylus? Longinus treats of animated, impassioned, energetic or if you will, elevated writing...."[12] Wordsworth's attempts to discover a substitute for the vague and popular sense of the term *sublime* occupied his thoughts chiefly during the period in which he was elaborating his distinction between fancy and imagination. His comments on the sublime and on imagination are almost always interchangeable, and the most important feature of all these comments is the religious associations of both concepts. At the close of his discourse on imagination in the Preface of 1815, he states his preference for "the prophetic and lyrical parts of the Holy Scriptures,

[12] *The Letters of William and Dorothy Wordsworth: The Later Years*, ed. Ernest de Selincourt (Oxford: Oxford University Press, 1939), I, 194; hereafter cited as *LY*. Coleridge also held that Longinus' subject was not the sublime, properly so called. See Thorpe, "Coleridge on the Sublime," *Wordsworth and Coleridge*, p. 219 n.

... the works of Milton," and of Spenser to "those of ancient Greece and Rome," because the classical writers were subjected "too much to the bondage of definite form."[13] About fifteen years earlier Coleridge had made the same contrast and drawn the same conclusion:

> The more I think, the more I am convinced that the greatest of differences is produced when in the one case the feelings are worked upon thro' the Imagination and the Imagination thro' definite Forms (i.e. the Religion of Greece and Rome); and in the other cases where the Feelings are worked upon by Hopes and Fears purely individual, and the Imagination is kept barren in definite Forms and only in cooperation with the Understanding labours after an obscure and indefinite Vastness—this is Christianity.[14]

He is even more explicit in a letter of 1802 to William Sotheby:

> It must occur to every Reader that the Greeks in their religious poems address always the Numina Loci, the Genii ... All natural Objects were *dead* ... but there was a Godkin or Goddessling *included* in each—In the Hebrew Poetry you will find nothing of this poor Stuff—as poor in genuine Imagination, as it is mean in Intellect—At best, it is but Fancy, or the aggregating Faculty of the mind— not *Imagination*, or the *modifying*, and *co-adunating*

[13] *PW*, II, 439.

[14] Quoted in Thorpe, "Coleridge on the Sublime," *Wordsworth and Coleridge*, p. 210. Thorpe says of this passage that "In other places Coleridge reveals an even more definite tendency to relate Christian belief to the sublime" (p. 211). For an account of the importance of Hebrew poetry to the development of romanticism, see Murray Roston, *Prophet and Poet: The Bible and the Growth of Romanticism* (Evanston: Northwestern University Press, 1965). As Roston illustrates, Wordsworth's and Coleridge's admiration for Hebrew over classical poetry was widely shared in the late eighteenth century.

Faculty. This the Hebrew Poets appear to me to have possessed beyond all others—& next to them the English.[15]

In some instances Wordsworth and Coleridge used the terms *sublime* and *imagination* practically as synonyms. Referring to Milton's description of Christ and his ten thousand Saints, "far off his coming shone" (*P.L.*, VI, 768), Coleridge cited it as an illustration of the highest sublime and Wordsworth as an illustration of imagination.[16] It is doubtful that Coleridge did in fact equate the two terms, but Wordsworth appears to have done so, and René Wellek remarks that Wordsworth's illustrations of imagination and fancy in the Preface of 1815 "lead to a rather naïve revival of the difference between the beautiful and sublime."[17] Wellek's adjective appears to me to be misapplied to Wordsworth. A topic so often discussed as the sublime was bound to be treated superficially more often than profoundly. Such had been its fate throughout the eighteenth century, until first Edmund Burke and then Immanuel Kant firmly established the sublime as a serious subject in aesthetics and psychology. It was to become the keystone of Romantic poetics, and for Wordsworth, however naïve his comments in the Preface may seem, the sublime was the test for the highest reaches in poetry.

A twentieth-century editor of Burke's essay on the sublime and beautiful implies that this work was a principal source of Wordsworth's and Coleridge's speculations.[18] For

[15] *Collected Letters of Samuel Taylor Coleridge*, ed. Earl Leslie Griggs (Oxford: Oxford University Press, 1956–1959), II, 865–866.

[16] Shawcross comments on this point in *BL*, II, 309.

[17] René Wellek, *A History of Modern Criticism* (New Haven: Yale University Press, 1955), II, 148.

[18] J. T. Boulton, ed., *A Philosophical Enquiry into the Origin of our Ideas of the Sublime and Beautiful* (London: Routledge and Kegan Paul, 1958), pp. xcix–ciii.

several reasons, however, evidence for Burke's direct
influence on either poet is unconvincing. According to
Burke, the essence of the sublime is its ability to rob "the
mind of all its powers of acting and reasoning," and the
emotion most capable of such effect is terror: "Indeed
terror is in all cases whatsoever, either more openly or
latently the ruling principle of the sublime."[19] Terror was
important for Wordsworth too, as any reader of *The
Prelude* knows, but he differs radically from Burke on the
final result of terror. For Burke it seems pretty much a dead
end, but for Wordsworth it is merely the stimulus to another
stage of perception. What most distinguishes Wordsworth's
and Coleridge's notions of the sublime from Burke's is the
insistence of the poets that only the Hebrew-Christian
religion truly merits the term. Though Burke naturally
speaks more warmly of the scriptures than of the writings of
pagan philosophers and poets, he seems to find if anything
less of terror, "the ruling principle of the sublime," in his
own religion, which has to some degree humanized God
by emphasizing His love for man.[20] Wordsworth and
Coleridge almost certainly derived some notions of the
sublime from Burke's *Enquiry*, but on the whole the
evidence of direct and significant influence is negligible;
and Coleridge is known to have commented that Burke's
essay was "a poor thing."[21]

There is no evidence at all that Wordsworth ever read

[19] *Ibid.*, pp. 57–58.
[20] *Ibid.*, pp. 69–70.
[21] Quoted by Boulton, p. cii. On Burke's essentially un-Romantic
view of the sublime, see Ernest Lee Tuveson, *The Imagination as a
Means of Grace* (Berkeley and Los Angeles: University of California
Press, 1960), pp. 166–174, and R. D. Havens, *The Mind of a Poet*
(Baltimore: Johns Hopkins Press, 1941), p. 52, n. 21.

the works of Kant or his school. Even Melvin Rader, who states that "there are grounds for inferring an important Kantian influence on Wordsworth," does not claim that this influence was direct.[22] It is not at all necessary, however, to prove direct influence. If it can be demonstrated that Coleridge's comments on the sublime were largely inspired by Kant's, the similarity between the views of Coleridge and Wordsworth on this subject will prepare for the next step—the attribution to Wordsworth of a primarily Kantian theory of the sublime. The value of establishing this similarity among the speculations of these three men is that both Kant and Coleridge were more articulate commentators on the metaphysical implications of the sublime than was Wordsworth, whose scattered remarks need the context that Kant and Coleridge can provide.

Scattered though they are, Wordsworth's comments on the sublime are more numerous than is usually supposed. Not all of them explicitly refer to it by name, but even where the term is not used it is applicable. The most formal and explicit of Wordsworth's published discussions of the sublime is in the often abused "Essay, Supplementary to the Preface," where it forms a part of his criticism of the popular concept of taste. He concedes that the faculty called taste has relevance to the judgment of some elements of the fine arts. With such matters as "proportion and congruity" the faculty we call taste may be trusted, "for in its intercourse with these the mind is *passive*." Of the higher achievements of art, however, taste is no fit judge:

> . . . the profound and the exquisite in feeling, the lofty and universal in thought and imagination; or, in ordinary

[22] Melvin Rader, *Presiding Ideas in Wordsworth's Poetry* (Seattle: University of Washington Press, 1931), p. 193.

language, the pathetic and the sublime;—are neither of them, accurately speaking, objects of a faculty which could ever without a sinking in the spirit of Nations have been designated by the metaphor—*Taste*.

The pathetic and the sublime in poetry cannot be referred to a passive faculty, "Because without the exertion of a co-operating *power* in the mind of the Reader, there can be no adequate sympathy with either of these emotions: without this auxiliary impulse, elevated or profound passion cannot exist." Later in the essay, Wordsworth repeats this last point in direct reference to the poetic imagination:

> Remember . . . that the medium through which, in poetry, the heart is to be affected, is language; a thing subject to endless fluctuations and arbitrary associations. The genius of the poet melts these down for his purpose; but they retain their shape and quality to him who is not capable of exerting, within his own mind, a corresponding energy.

In other words, the imagination has the power to confer, to abstract, to modify, to shape, and to create—but these powers are ineffectual when they fail to find in the reader of poetry at least a dim echo of similar powers. To one for whom a primrose is and remains nothing more than a primrose, the experience of the sublime is impossible. No wonder then that, demanding so much from his readers, a poet who attempts to convey such experiences "must reconcile himself for a season to few and scattered hearers":

> And for the sublime,—if we consider what are the cares that occupy the passing day, and how remote is the practice and the course of life from the sources of sublimity, in the soul of Man, can it be wondered that there is little existing

152

preparation for a poet charged with a new mission to extend its kingdom, and to augment and spread its enjoyments?[23]

This essay is often peremptorily branded an exercise in self-justification and as peremptorily ignored, but it contains a careful, lucid statement of Wordsworth's theory of the value of poetry, and is in many ways a better source of information concerning his philosophic and moral beliefs about poetry than the more technical preface which it is in part intended to supplement. Wordsworth's account of the process of communication between poet and reader is not unique, but it should be remembered when we are tempted to accept uncritically the distinction between the Romantic poets and their predecessors on grounds of "private" and "public" poetry. For Wordsworth communication with the reader was not a subject to be referred merely—or even primarily—to rhetorical principles and techniques. It was rather a moral and philosophic matter, a part of his theory of the experience of the sublime and the attempt to render that experience in poetry that would appeal to "the sources of sublimity, in the soul of Man."[24]

In a letter of 1824 Wordsworth answered Landor's attack against religious works by confessing that he had little use for any other kind: "I mean to say that, unless in those passages where things are lost in each other, and

[23] *PW*, II, 427–429. In an essay "Upon Epitaphs" Wordsworth wrote that the communication of "those primary sensations of the human heart, which are the vital springs of sublime and pathetic composition" depends upon corresponding sensations "in the inner cell of the mind to whom it is addressed." *The Prose Works of William Wordsworth*, ed. Alexander B. Grosart (London, 1876), II, 48; hereafter cited as *Prose*.

[24] *PW*, II, 428.

limits vanish, and aspirations are raised, I read with something too much like indifference—but all great poets are in
this view powerful Religionists. . . ."[25] The experience in
which "limits vanish and aspirations are raised" is an
experience of the sublime, and all *great* poets—that is, poets
who communicate in their works these sublime experiences
—are religionists because the experience of the sublime is
above all religious.[26] For this reason, matters of "proportion
and congruity" can be referred to a faculty less exalted than
the imagination, since such considerations belong not
to the sublime, but to the beautiful.[27] The tendency to elevate
the sublime at the expense of the beautiful is a prominent
characteristic of Kant's discussion of these terms in his

[25] *LY*, I, 134–135.

[26] In revising this chapter I found very helpful a recent study
emphasizing the transcendental faith of Romantic poets, James
Benziger's *Images of Eternity* (Carbondale: Southern Illinois University
Press, 1962). In a brief but illuminating section called "Sublimity
and Immortality" (pp. 52–65), Benziger remarks that Wordsworth's
"sublime moments" recall Kant "rather than Longinus or Burke."

[27] For a perceptive discussion of the relationship between the
beautiful and sublime and the mature and immature imagination, see
Kenneth MacLean, "Levels of Imagination in Wordsworth's *Prelude*
(1805)," *PQ*, XXXVIII (1959), 385–400. The tendency to identify
taste as the faculty for appreciating beauty, and some higher power
for responding to the sublime was Wordsworth's (and Kant's)
heritage from eighteenth-century reactions against strict application
of the rules. Thus, Horace Walpole writes, "One must have taste to be
sensible of the beauties of Grecian architecture; one only wants
passions to feel Gothic"; and we move still closer to Romantic
doctrine with the following remark from one of the early discourses
of Joshua Reynolds, whose influence on Wordsworth's aesthetics has
not been sufficiently emphasized: ". . . Raffaelle had more Taste and
Fancy; Michel Angelo, more Genius and Imagination. The one
excelled in beauty, the other in energy. Michel Angelo has more of the
poetical Inspiration; his ideas are vast and sublime . . . ." *Anecdotes of
Painting in England* (London, 1871), p. 70; Discourse V, December
10, 1772, in *Discourses Delivered . . . by Sir Joshua Reynolds*, ed.
Roger Fry (London: Seeley and Co., 1905), p. 122.

Critique of Judgement. As Barrows Dunham observes, for Kant "Emotion in the experience of the sublime is relatively safe, because it is grounded in morality ... but emotion such as may be aroused by beauty tends to vitiate the experience by degenerating into sentimentality."[28] The basis for Kant's preference for the sublime over the beautiful is his association of the sublime with reason (*Vernunft*) and the beautiful with understanding (*Verstand*).

The distinction between a higher and lower intellectual faculty is the clearest point of contact between the thought of Kant and Wordsworth. Rader comments that it is "very likely that the discrimination between the higher and lower reason was derived from Kant through the mediation of Coleridge," and that "Wordsworth, like Kant, regards imagination as closely bound to the higher reason."[29] And when John Jones remarks that Wordsworth viewed "the commanding of expressive forms as an exercise of practical reason ... ," he is applying Kantian terminology to Wordsworth.[30] The most emphatic statement of the similarity between the theories of Kant and Wordsworth is that of Monk, who discusses the larger question of Kant's role in the Romantic movement as follows:

> This is not to say that Kant created the romantic age, but that his philosophy and the art of the romantics are symptoms of a changed point of view. .... Argument by analogy

[28] Barrows Dunham, "Kant's Theory of Aesthetic Form," in *The Heritage of Kant*, ed. George Tapley Whitney and David F. Bowers (Princeton: Princeton University Press, 1939), p. 369.

[29] Rader, *Presiding Ideas*, pp. 193, 168. In a letter of 1811, Wordsworth speaks of the need in his day for "a new course of education, a higher tone of moral feeling, more of the grandeur of the Imaginative faculties, and less of the petty processes of the unfeeling and purblind understanding ..." (*MY*, I, 440).

[30] John Jones, *The Egotistical Sublime* (London: Chatto and Windus, 1954), p. viii.

is confessedly weak, but the nature of this change can be indicated by saying that it is possible to maintain that there is a general similarity between the point of view of the *Critique of Judgment* and the *Prelude.* . . .[31]

Such an interpretation need not imply that Wordsworth was a conscious follower of Kant, or even that he was a conscious follower of a Kantian Coleridge. Indeed, one recent book on Wordsworth makes no assertion of any such influence, yet demonstrates convincingly that there are striking similarities between the ideas, and even the language, of Wordsworth and one of Kant's disciples.[32]

Wordsworth's comments on the sublime and the beautiful show that he customarily associates the former with imagination and the higher reason, the latter, with fancy and understanding. The experience of the beautiful is mild and leaves the mind in a state of peaceful rest; it is, therefore, an experience purely of pleasure. The experience of the sublime, on the other hand, produces not rest but agitation, creating a state in which pain and pleasure are inextricably combined, so that, in fact, it is only by the initial feeling of pain that the ultimate pleasure can be engendered. In a letter to his sister, in which he describes his first tour through the Alps, Wordsworth pauses to reflect on the contrast between the two kinds of scenes he has witnessed:

> It was impossible not to contrast that repose, that complacency of spirit, produced by these lovely scenes [of Lake Como], with the sensations I had experienced two or three days before, in passing the Alps. At the lake of

[31] Monk, *The Sublime*, p. 5.
[32] E. D. Hirsch, Jr., *Wordsworth and Schelling: A Typological Study of Romanticism* (New Haven: Yale University Press, 1960).

Como, my mind ran through a thousand dreams of happiness, which might be enjoyed upon its banks, if heightened by conversation and the exercise of the social affections. Among the more awful scenes of the Alps, I had not a thought of man, or a single created being; my whole soul was turned to him who produced the terrible majesty before me.[33]

Immediately preceding and immediately following this passage, he consistently speaks of "sublime and beautiful" scenery, arranging the sights into these two groups.

The most important point in Wordsworth's contrast is that the experience of beautiful scenes permits the imagination to form pictures in the mind, pictures capable of rather clear translation in words; but the feelings produced by the terrible and awful scenes among the Alps leave him without definite images. The very essence of the sublime is that it defeats the powers of man, thus forcing him to admit the presence of a greater power. Speaking of the proper subject of the imagination in the Preface of 1815, Wordsworth remarks that "the Soul may fall away from it, not being able to sustain its grandeur; but, if once felt and acknowledged, by no act of any other faculty of the mind can it be relaxed, impaired, or diminished."[34] The immediate effect of the sublime is to deprive the imagination of its ability to create adequate images. It is only later that some means can be found to render the experience with any clarity. For Kant the sublime is primarily a moral experience because the

---

[33] EL, pp. 32–33. Cf. Thorpe's statement of Coleridge's similar view: "The effect [of sublime experiences], as we may infer it from passages in the 'Marginalia,' is not rest in the object, but retreat of the mind upon itself in imaginative contemplations of infinity" ("Coleridge on the Sublime," Wordsworth and Coleridge, p. 203).

[34] PW, II, 441–442.

mind is pushed to its limits; it is not in repose, not passive and complacent, but driven to seek some means of rendering its experience lucidly, so that it is "incited to abandon sensibility, and employ itself upon ideas involving higher finality."[35] Wordsworth's expression of this belief differs from Kant's chiefly in its traditional Christian terminology:

> Faith was given to man that his affections, detached from the treasures of time, might be inclined to settle upon those of eternity. . . . The religious man values what he sees chiefly as an "imperfect shadowing forth" of what he is incapable of seeing. The concerns of religion refer to indefinite objects, and are too weighty for the mind to support them without relieving itself by resting a great part of the burthen upon words and symbols. The commerce between Man and his Maker cannot be carried on but by a process where much is represented in little, and the Infinite Being accommodates himself to a finite capacity. In all this may be perceived the affinity between religion and poetry . . . between religion . . . submitting herself to circumscription, and reconciled to substitutions; and poetry—ethereal and transcendent, yet incapable to sustain her existence without sensuous incarnation.[36]

It is impossible to reconcile this statement with Arthur Beatty's view that for Wordsworth "imagination is simple truth to experience, to the real experience which we all know; not to some transcendental, far-away, or Utopian, or supposedly ideal truth, but to the truth of the world in

[35] Immanuel Kant, *Critique of Aesthetic Judgement*, trans. James Creed Meredith (Oxford: Oxford University Press, 1911), p. 92. The affinity of Kant's philosophy for the Romantic poets is understandable, for, as R. W. Bretall remarks, "the background of his doctrine of the sublime lies mainly in the literary and artistic *criticism* of the . . . period" ("Kant's Theory of the Sublime," *The Heritage of Kant*, p. 380).

[36] From "Essay, Supplementary to the Preface," *PW*, II, 412.

which we live."[37] On the contrary, the ultimate concern of the imagination is precisely with the transcendental and the ideal; its home is "with infinitude, and only there." Religion is like poetry in that each must manifest itself by means not equal to its intrinsic worth; each must stoop to reveal to man "the hiding places" of his power, his "possible sublimity."

How close to Wordsworth's statement just quoted are Kant's comments on the sublime can be seen in this passage from the *Critique of Judgement*:

> Those forms . . . as secondary representations of the imagination . . . the concept of which, as an idea of reason, cannot be adequately presented . . . do not, like *logical attributes*, represent what lies in our concepts of the sublimity and majesty of creation, but . . . [are] something that gives the imagination an incentive to spread its flight over a whole host of kindred representations that provoke more thought than admits of expression in a concept determined by words.[38]

Wordsworth, Coleridge, and Kant all believed that this experience is too great for man to express in ordinary discourse. In Kant's theory, of course, the faculty of concepts is the understanding, and these concepts can be clearly expressed. The ideas of reason, on the other hand, are not capable of translation. Because man can present these ideas only as symbols, the poet assumes special importance in the doctrines of the transcendentalists. In Schelling's theory, for example, the imagination is considered higher than reason, able to penetrate to the noumenal

[37] Arthur Beatty, *William Wordsworth: His Doctrine and Art in their Historical Relations* (3rd ed.; Madison: University of Wisconsin Press, 1960), p. 192.
[38] Kant, *Critique of Aesthetic Judgement*, p. 177.

reality, of which, in Kant's theory, no faculty can deliver ideas of *objective* validity.[39] And though Coleridge refuses to place imagination above what he calls reason, he too refuses to admit that insight into ultimate reality is denied to man and so claims for the "higher reason" the power to produce objectively valid ideas.[40]

In a letter of 1825, Wordsworth expresses the belief that "we shall never see clearly into this subject [the sublime] unless we turn from objects to laws...," the same laws, surely, that he refers to in the Preface of 1800: "the primary laws of our nature: chiefly, as far as regards the manner in which we associate ideas in a state of excitement." And this excitement is not the sort induced by "the application of gross and violent stimulants," but that agitation and unrest and awe with which the imagination responds to the sublime.[41] It is through Wordsworth's theory of the sublime experience that we should approach his famous declaration concerning his poems in the Preface to *Lyrical Ballads*, that "the feeling therein developed gives importance to the action and situation, and not the action and situation to the feeling."[42] Repeatedly Wordsworth emphasizes that the value of the experience of the sublime is its power to turn the imagination from the senses to that which lies beyond their grasp. Because the result of this experience is to permit the imagination to escape the rule of the senses, it follows that the usual setting for the sublime is one in which the senses are in some way frustrated, when "the light of

[39] See John Watson, *Schelling's Transcendental Idealism* (Chicago, 1882), *passim*; and Judson S. Lyon, "Romantic Psychology and the Inner Senses: Coleridge," *PMLA*, LXXXI (1966), 255–256.

[40] See *BL*, I, xlii–xliv.

[41] *LY*, I, 195; *PW*, II, 386, 389.

[42] *PW*, II, 388–389.

sense / Goes out, but with a flash that has revealed / The invisible world" (*Prelude*, VI, 600–602). In a letter of 1811 to Sir George Beaumont, Wordsworth describes such a setting:

> It was about the hour of sunset, and the sea was perfectly calm, and in a quarter where its surface was indistinguishable from the western sky, hazy, and luminous with the setting Sun, appeared a tall sloop-rigged vessel, magnified by the atmosphere through which it was viewed, and seeming rather to hang in the air than to float upon the waters.[43]

At the close of the passage, Wordsworth compares this scene to Milton's description of Satan's awesome size as "a Fleet descried far off at sea." Four years later he cites this image in the Preface of 1815 as an example of the power of imagination, a power "proceeding from, and governed by, a sublime consciousness of the soul in her own mighty and almost divine powers."[44] The soul is given insight into these powers when the senses have been strained to their limit and forced to abdicate, so that the higher faculties can strive to satisfy the demands of an experience transcending sense.

In his *Guide to the Lakes*, Wordsworth argues that because sublimity does not depend on the "actual magnitude" of objects, the mountains of the Lake Country are, under certain conditions, as capable of evoking the sublime experience as are the greater Alps. He is quite specific about these conditions: "... the resemblance [between the two regions] would be still more perfect on those days when vapours, resting upon, and floating around the summits, leave the elevation of the mountains less dependent upon

[43] *MY*, II, 470.
[44] *PW*, II, 439.

the eye than on the imagination."[45] An entry in one of Dorothy Wordsworth's journals expresses the same idea: "... an imperfect light helps to set the imagination a stirring."[46] It is the power of the sublime to set the imagination in motion that dominates Wordsworth's reflections on this kind of experience.

The clearest evidence of the similarity between the reflections on the sublime of Wordsworth and his sister is this 1803 entry from one of her journals:

> It seldom happens that mountains in a very clear air look exceedingly high, but these, though we could see the whole of them to their very summits, appeared to me more majestic in their own nakedness than our imaginations could have conceived them to be, had they been half hidden by clouds, yet showing some of their highest pinnacles. They were such forms as Milton might be supposed to have had in his mind when he applied to Satan that sublime expression—
>
> *His stature reached the sky.*[47]

Wordsworth, of course, was to illustrate the boundlessness

[45] *Prose*, II, 293. Wordsworth later clarified this passage in a letter written in 1828: "In the book on the Lakes ... I content myself with saying, that after a certain point of elevation the effect of mountains depends much more upon their form than upon their absolute height. This point, which ought to have been defined, is the one to which fleecy clouds (not thin watery vapours) are accustomed to descend" (*LY*, I, 335–336). This more exact description is important because "thin watery vapours" would not adequately frustrate the senses in their attempt to grasp the scene as a whole and thereby limit it to the merely visual.

[46] *Journals of Dorothy Wordsworth*, ed. Ernest de Selincourt (New York: The Macmillan Company, 1941), II, 38; hereafter cited as *Journals*.

[47] *Journals*, I, 331–332.

of products of the imagination with this same quotation from Milton.

In the passage just quoted, Dorothy explains that this scene is exceptional in that it does not contain the usual features and circumstances attributed to scenes that evoke sublimity. The characteristic setting for the sublime is that which Wordsworth describes in the passages previously quoted, and it is this setting to which Dorothy customarily applies the term *sublime*. I shall quote several such passages from the journals, because a recognition of these settings should prepare us for Wordsworth's poetic renderings of them and should clarify the peculiar nature of his symbols of eternity, which resist our usual approaches to poetic symbolism:

> The whole was indeed a strange mixture of soothing and restless images, of images inviting to rest, and others hurrying the fancy[48] away into an activity still more pleasing than repose; yet, intricate and homeless, that is, without lasting abidingplace for the mind, as the prospect was, there was no perplexity. . . . Wherever we looked, it was with a delightful feeling that there was something beyond.
>
> . . . the musings upon time and eternity which must visit all but the most unthinking minds in a solitude like this, surrounded by objects so sublime.
>
> I hardly can conceive a place of more solitary aspect than the lake of Chiavenna: and the whole of the prospect in that direction is characterized by melancholy sublimity . . . .
>
> Above the head of the Stream [the Arve], fields of snow, scattered over with rocks, ascend to the fantastic or sublime masses of granite, which cannot be looked at

[48] The context suggests that *imagination* would have been the more appropriate term.

163

without sometimes recalling images of castles, spires . . . , though their bulk, their number, their sublime stations, forbid all but *transient* thoughts unconnected with lonely Nature, and the first mysterious Cause of whatever we behold.[49]

Abstracting common elements from these and similar passages, we can characterize the usual setting of sublime experiences as one in which the senses are forced to yield to the imagination. Usually this situation is produced by a scene whose elements are indistinct, in which boundaries and limits seem not to exist so that the senses are unable to present to the understanding the distinct and discrete sensations which alone are within its province. Usually too the scene is viewed in solitude, away from the distractions that would defeat the imagination by providing the senses with material to keep them active.[50] In such settings as this, Wordsworth experienced the visionary insights to which his best poetry attempts to give form. All the elements which I have just discussed are present in the following passage from *The Prelude*, in which Wordsworth recounts the birth in him of the mysterious experiences that inspired his greatest attempts in poetry:

> for I would walk alone,
> Under the quiet stars, and at that time
> Have felt whate'er there is of power in sound
> To breathe an elevated mood, by form
> Or image unprofaned; and I would stand,
> If the night blackened with a coming storm,

[49] *Journals*, I, 253; II, 105–106, 245, 285.

[50] "Grand thoughts," says Wordsworth, "are most naturally and most fitly conceived in solitude . . ." (*PW*, II, 429). In *Wordsworth's Anti-Climax* (Cambridge: Harvard University Press, 1935), Willard L. Sperry writes that "The essence of solitariness is with him an immunity to sense experiences" (p. 193).

Beneath some rock, listening to notes that are
The ghostly language of the ancient earth,
Or make their dim abode in distant winds.
Thence did I drink the visionary power;
And deem not profitless those fleeting moods
Of shadowy exultation: not for this
That they are kindred to our purer mind
And intellectual life; but that the soul,
Remembering how she felt, but what she felt
Remembering not, retains an obscure sense
Of possible sublimity, whereto
With growing faculties she doth aspire,
With faculties still growing, feeling still
That whatsoever point they gain, they yet
Have something to pursue.   (II, 302–322)

Later in this passage he says of such experiences:

Oft in these moments such a holy calm
Would overspread my soul, that bodily eyes
Were utterly forgotten, and what I saw
Appeared like something in myself, a dream,
A prospect in the mind.   (II, 348–352)

Implicit in these lines is a confession that we must recognize before we can hope to understand Wordsworth's symbols. The confession is this: because these experiences of pure transcendence are "by form or image unprofaned," they cannot be perfectly translated. Thus Wordsworth's best poetry is necessarily a compromise between the desire to achieve the impossible, to preserve unviolated the visionary experience of transcendence, and the realization that such experiences are beyond the power of man's description. His awareness of the limitations of expression explains the almost bitter discourse in the supplementary essay of 1815 on the inadequacy of language to communicate our profoundest intuitions. Wordsworth is not, as some critics have charged, merely rationalizing his own loss of power, but rather insisting that even when he is at the height of his powers there are experiences which leave man's faculties "feeling still / That whatsoever point they gain, they yet / Have something to pursue." In describing the dilemma of twentieth-century poets, Wallace Stevens also described the obverse of Romantic faith in poetry and the poet, for Wordsworth no less than Stevens knew that our world is one of "flawed words and stubborn sounds."[51]

Coleridge, following the course assigned to him in the plan of *Lyrical Ballads*, attempts to express the reality beyond sense by circumventing the senses and appealing directly to an imagination free from sense. But Wordsworth, perhaps because of the influence of associationism, could not use Coleridge's approach, for he believed that though poetry is "ethereal and transcendent," it is nevertheless "incapable to sustain her existence without sensuous incarnation." It is difficult to see how it can be argued that Wordsworth preferred "the immediate simple processes of the mind and imagination, as opposed to the supposedly higher 'intuitive,' and 'transcendental' ones."[52] Poetry *is* "ethereal and transcendent," Wordsworth says, and it is not preference that keeps man from expressing the intuitive and transcendental. Rather it is the inadequacy of language that prevents man from expressing those few fleeting glimpses of vision granted him. And the very limitation of language gives it a terrifying importance: "Words are too

[51] Wallace Stevens, "The Poems of our Climate," from *The Collected Poems of Wallace Stevens* (New York: Alfred A. Knopf, 1964).
[52] Beatty, *William Wordsworth*, p. 126.

awful an instrument for good and evil, to be trifled with; they hold above all other external powers a dominion over thoughts."[53]

All symbolism is born of the compromise that defines the limits of human expression. No art is more circumscribed by this limitation than poetry and no group of poets was more aware of it than the Romantics. "Symbolic presentation," Kant wrote, yields concepts "to which no sensible intuition can be adequate." As an attempt to bridge the gulf between experience and expression, symbolism never achieves complete success. Indeed, when it is most nearly successful, as in poetry, its failure is the more apparent. The Romantic faith that a poem is organic, has a life of its own, is the stuff of tragedy. The poem is somehow beyond the control of its author: it will outlive him, even usurp him, asserting its right to say more, less, or other than its creator intended.[54] Wordsworth's poems of imagination are of this kind. In them the symbolism is meant to suggest not arbitrary artistic contrivances, but true statements of the relationship between Nature and mind. The poems are attempts to render without distortion the truths of experiences that lie beyond the reach of abstract thought and rational discourse. Each of these poems, whatever its degree of purely aesthetic success, fits Coleridge's definition of "the grandest efforts of poetry," wherein the intended

[53] *Prose Works of William Wordsworth*, ed. William Knight (London, 1896), II, 177.

[54] On the Romantic poets' obsession with the limits of language, see esp. Frank Kermode, *Romantic Image* (London: Routledge and Kegan Paul Ltd., 1957), p. 47, *et passim*; David Perkins, *Wordsworth and the Poetry of Sincerity* (Cambridge: Harvard University Press, 1964), esp. chapt. IV, "The Adequacy of Language"; and Earl R. Wasserman, *The Subtler Language* (Baltimore: Johns Hopkins Press, 1959), *passim*.

result is "the substitution of a sublime feeling of the un-
imaginable for a mere image."[55] The key word is "un-
imaginable." A true Wordsworthian poem of imagination
offers no detachable symbols, but a feeling from the whole
that is itself a symbol.

In some poems of imagination there are images that
appear to be symbols in the popular sense of the term. The
song of "The Solitary Reaper" so dominates the poem, or
seems to, that it has understandably been detached from its
context and given an exact rational meaning: the poem,
says one critic, "is constructed on the contradictions in the
girl's song which is both natural and mysterious, near and
distant, symbolic of eternal beauty."[56] Such a translation of
the song's meaning falsifies an otherwise acute interpretation
of the poem by shifting the emphasis from the speaker to a
single image somehow separate from him. I would argue
that here as in all Wordsworth's poems of imagination there
is no symbol that can be derived from a single object. The
symbolism of these poems reflects Wordsworth's approach
to the sublime through laws of mind rather than through
objects or sensations.

The importance of the song in "The Solitary Reaper" is
its power to extend the senses to their limits until they
relinquish their rule to the imagination. The song itself is
not the symbol, but its vehicle, and the symbol is the
imaginative process by which the song acquires extra-
sensible significance to the poet whose imagination is set in

[55] *Coleridge's Shakespearean Criticism*, ed. Thomas M. Raysor (2nd
ed.; London: J. M. Dent and Sons Ltd., 1961), II, 103–104.
[56] Elizabeth Nitchie, "Form in Romantic Poetry," in *The Major
English Romantic Poets*, ed. Clarence D. Thorpe, Carlos Baker, and
Bennett Weaver (Carbondale: Southern Illinois University Press,
1957), p. 14.

motion by it. If we must choose a name for the symbols generated in this type of poem, we can not do better than to adopt Wordsworth's own name for them—"The types and symbols of Eternity, / Of first, and last, and midst, and without end" (*Prelude*, VI, 639–640). The principal significance of the reaper's song is not the song itself ("Whate'er the theme, the Maiden sang") but what the imagination is able to make of its object—a thing of timeless presence, hence an image of eternity ("As if her song could have no ending"), just as the greeting of another solitary maid, in a companion poem, seems "a sound / Of something without place or bound."[57]

The imagination makes of the song a token of the timelessness of time and the boundlessness of space, reflecting the belief that space and time are creations of the mind, not data passively accepted by it. Because the words of the song are in a language the speaker does not understand, his imagination can divest it of all limitations, so that like the cuckoo's song or the song of Keats' nightingale, it sums up in an infinite moment of imaginative activity all the elemental passions ever experienced, all that "has been, and may be again." The second stanza extends the song spatially, from "Arabian sands" to "the farthest Hebrides"; the third dramatizes its relevance through all ranges of human experience and in all times, from "old, unhappy, far-off things, / And battles long ago" to "Familiar matter of to-day / Some natural sorrow, loss, or pain."[58]

The speaker's speculations about the matter of the song

[57] "Stepping Westward," ll. 13–14.

[58] Keats' "Ode to a Nightingale," probably indebted to "The Solitary Reaper," employs the same rich symbolism. In transforming the bird's song into a symbol of eternity, Keats extends its implications so as to embrace all ranks of men (from emperor to clown) and all

remain speculations, but the permanent importance of the imagination's handling of the experience is assured. Whatever may happen to the girl or her song as objects of the senses, the imagination has its symbol as evidence of an insight into the mystical unity of life. And this is why the song lives beyond the brief narrative of the poem, why in the closing lines the speaker tells us not that the song has ceased, but rather that it "was heard no more." His soul expanded by an experience of the sublime, he can continue on his way, bearing in his *heart* an experience that has been transformed into a symbol of infinitude.[59] At this point we may recall Wordsworth's statement that the elevation of man's nature, produced by experiences that lift the soul out of the world of the senses, is "a presumptive evidence of a future state" and gives him "a title to partake of its holiness."[60] This last remark is an echo of the statement in "Stepping Westward" that the young girl's greeting "seemed to be / A kind of *heavenly* destiny" which "seemed to give me spiritual right / To travel through that region bright." The experience of the sublime is itself a symbol, the promise that man's "being's heart and home, / Is with

times—historical (the "ancient days" of emperor and clown), Biblical ("the sad heart of Ruth," herself a solitary reaper), and legendary ("faery lands forlorn"). That Wordsworth's poem ends in joyous affirmation and Keats' in doubt is at once a matter of personality and of the crisis of doubt in imaginative vision that overcame the second generation of Romantic poets.

59 Wordsworth's use of the word *heart*, in both poetry and prose, shows that it had more significance for him than as a symbol for one of the Hartleian ages of man. Like Coleridge he undoubtedly associated it with its traditional Christian meaning as the organ of faith, the faculty to which religious truths are said to appeal directly. It is obviously used in this sense in *The Prelude* lines, "our being's heart and home, / Is with infinitude, and only there" (VI, 604–605). See Lyon, "Romantic Psychology," *PMLA*, LXXXI, 253.

60 *PW*, II, 412.

infinitude, and only there." All those poems that I have classified as poems of imagination are affirmations of this belief. Each evolves a symbol of infinitude under the impetus of an experience of the sublime, in which the soul reaches through sense to something transcending sense.

Perhaps the clearest description of this mode of poetic symbolism is Helen Darbishire's comment on "My Heart Leaps Up": "He leaves the image to do its work with no explanation. He simply tells us his experience: that images which have stirred his feelings vitally, continue to move through his mind with a lasting life."[61]

This remark will serve to introduce a characteristic of Wordsworth's poetry that has consistently troubled both his critics and his admirers. By far the most famous commentary on this point is the following passage from the *Biographia*, in which the same poem is discussed:

> Nothing is more likely . . . than that a vivid image or visual spectrum . . . may become the link of association in recalling the feelings and images that had accompanied the original impression. But if we describe this in such lines, as
>> "They flash upon that inward eye,
>> Which is the bliss of solitude!"
> in what words shall we describe the joy of retrospection, when the images and virtuous actions of a whole well-spent life, pass before that conscience which is indeed the *inward* eye: which is indeed "*the bliss of solitude?*" Assuredly we seem to sink most abruptly, not to say burlesquely, and almost as in a *medly*, from this couplet to—
>> "And then my heart with pleasure fills,
>> And dances with the *daffodils*."   (II, 109–110)

[61] Helen Darbishire, "Wordsworth's Significance for Us," in *The Major English Romantic Poets*, p. 75.

Such criticism as this should make us hesitate to turn habitually to Coleridge for help in discovering the "essential" Wordsworth.[62] At best, his remarks on this poem are a reflection of his increasing tendency to refer everything to traditional Christian dogma. His equating Wordsworth's (or Mrs. Wordsworth's) "inward eye" with the conscience is of a piece with his translation of Kant's *Understanding* (*Verstand*) as "the mind of the flesh" and Kant's Categorical Imperative as the Golden Rule.[63] At worst one is tempted to accept Crabb Robinson's testimony that Coleridge sometimes judged Wordsworth "under personal feelings of unkindness."[64] The *Biographia* is still our best source of perceptive criticism of Wordsworth's poetry, but like the poems it discusses, its quality is uneven. Coleridge was a man and a critic of very strong ideas, and he had no reservations about limiting his praise of Wordsworth's poetry to the kind that satisfied the demands of his own theory of imagination. Srikumar Banerjee's generalization about Coleridge's criticism seems to me quite valid: "He nobly appraises the more obvious excellencies of Wordsworth's poetry; but he seems never to be in full sympathy with this strain of mysticism in the greater poet."[65] It is not

[62] In his Introduction to a group of essays on "Wordsworth and his Nineteenth-Century Critics," Derek Stanford calls Coleridge a "classical," that is, a "traditional" critic. *Tribute to Wordsworth*, ed. Muriel Spark and Derek Stanford (London and New York: Wingate, 1950), p. 24. David Ferry also characterizes Coleridge's judgment of Wordsworth's "mental bombast" as the viewpoint of a classicist. *The Limits of Mortality* (Middletown: Wesleyan University Press, 1959), pp. 5–7.

[63] Shedd, *Works of Coleridge*, I, 255; *The Literary Remains*, ed. Henry Nelson Coleridge (London, 1839), IV, 425.

[64] Morley, *Henry Crabb Robinson*, I, 288.

[65] Srikumar Banerjee, *Critical Theories and Poetic Practice in the "Lyrical Ballads"* (London: Williams and Norgate Ltd., 1931), p. 13.

that Coleridge was incapable of understanding mystical insights, but that the kind he understood is so different from Wordsworth's. From the beginning, in the division of labor decided upon for *Lyrical Ballads*, Coleridge sought to embody his visions independently of actual sense impressions. He could not understand that Wordsworth was able to achieve sublimity only through sense experience, by means of objects like daffodils and clouds, by means of sounds, like the hoots of owls.

But Coleridge is by no means alone in his attacks on Wordsworth's "mental bombast." In a review of the *Poems* of 1807, a critic for *The Annual Review and History of Literature* complains of this same fault, and uses for illustration the same poem that Coleridge was to cite later:

> When a man endeavours to make his reader enter into an association that exists in his own mind between daffodils waving in the wind, and laughter—or to teach him to see something very fine in the fancy of crowning a little rock with snow-drops, he fails, and is sure to fail; for it would be strange indeed if any one besides himself ever formed association[s], so capricious and entirely arbitrary.[66]

A criticism of the edition of 1815 in *The Quarterly Review* makes essentially the same point. Wordsworth should, says this reviewer, condescend to feel as other men feel, if his readers are to understand him. And although it is good to feel rapture over "the great and striking features of nature," one should not feel "*emotions which lie too deep for tears even with respect to the meanest flower that blows,*" nor should he "*cry for nothing* . . . over every ordinary object and every common-place occurrence. . . ." This objection, of course,

[66] Quoted in Elsie Smith, *An Estimate of William Wordsworth by his Contemporaries* (Oxford: Basil Blackwell, 1932), p. 91.

begs the question, because to Wordsworth, and to the audience he sought, these occurrences are not at all common-place in the sense in which the reviewer uses the term. This reviewer, indeed, would banish from poetry the creative imagination as Wordsworth conceived of it, for he would have it that the poet should awaken in his readers' minds "the particular feelings and emotions with which the various objects of his art are naturally associated."[67]

Wordsworth's critics, contemporary and modern, have constantly been vexed by his insistence on writing serious poetry about apparently mean or trivial objects. The best known of the contemporary commentators on his poetry—Coleridge, Crabb Robinson, and Hazlitt—all expressed their objections to this characteristic. Robinson, for example, found "good sense" in Leigh Hunt's remarks in *The Feast of Poets* "on the unworthy objects which Words-worth sometimes selects," and even agreed with the com-ment of the reviewer of *Peter Bell* in the *Eclectic Review* "that to dwell as Wordsworth does on the meanest of objects, exerting on them all the force of his intellect, evinces a sort of insanity."[68] He also seems to have agreed with Coleridge, who charged that "with malice prepense" Wordsworth "cast his reflexion on objects that do not naturally excite it."[69]

More recent critics have generally taken a middle position on Wordsworth's choice of subjects. Banerjee, for example, says of poems like "The Thorn" and "Goody Blake and

[67] *The Quarterly Review*, XIV (1815), 208–209. The reviewer also reveals his lack of qualifications by misreading a crucial line of the Ode, confusing, as its author certainly did not, *thoughts* and *emotions*.

[68] Morley, *Henry Crabb Robinson*, I, 138, 234.

[69] *Blake, Coleridge, Wordsworth, Lamb, Etc.*, ed. Edith J. Morley (Manchester: Manchester University Press, 1922), p. 31.

Harry Gill," works that Wordsworth valued much more highly than have his critics, that "the mystic importance of the subjects misled the poet as to the precise quality and extent of their imaginative appeal, and . . . he mistook his own feelings raised spontaneously by the subjects for feelings created by his own art in the mind of the reader..."[70] And Raleigh remarks that *Peter Bell* suffers from the same "stubborn naturalism," the same "unflinching determination to see things as they are, without ornament and without sophistication [which] produced the great poems of the next few years."[71] John Jones agrees with Raleigh that "the most vital quality of Wordsworth's mind . . . its literalness" is both the strength and the weakness of his poetry: "Everything, for him, was what it was, and it was not anything else: the thing done or suffered, the thing seen or heard or read, touched him because it was so. In its being so he saw it as somehow self-guaranteeing—this was the heart of his naturalistic optimism."[72]

Of Wordsworth's "Poems of the Imagination," Crabb Robinson remarks that they "are of such characteristic quality, that whoever has read them without enjoyment should not be teased with any recommendation to read more." On another occasion, he refers to a principal characteristic of such poems, "the opposition between the apparent strength of the passion and the insignificance of the object" which gives rise to that passion. In both instances, Robinson's remarks are perceptive. The best of the "Poems of the Imagination" are productions of a mode

[70] Banerjee, *Critical Theories*, p. 124.
[71] Walter Raleigh, *Wordsworth* (2nd impress.; London: Edward Arnold, 1903), pp. 78–79.
[72] Jones, *The Egotistical Sublime*, pp. 15–16.

of poetry that we recognize as distinctively Wordsworthian, and a prominent feature of this mode is the apparent disparity between objects and incidents described and the poet's reaction to them. To understand better Wordsworth's choice of subjects, we must constantly bear in mind that, as Robinson tells us, Wordsworth "valued ... [his poems] only according to the powers of mind they presupposed in the writer or excited in the hearer."[73] This is essentially the point that Havens makes in his distinction between the theories of imagination of Wordsworth and Coleridge:

> It seems, therefore, that Coleridge thought of the imagination chiefly as it relates to poetry and thus regarded it as a conscious activity of the mind; Wordsworth, on the other hand, usually conceived of it as the transformation wrought within the mind rather than any expression of such a transformation in a work of art.[74]

This is a penetrating comment, and it goes far toward explaining Wordsworth's insistence on writing profound poetry about objects and events apparently insignificant in themselves. He did so, we can assume, because for him the mere fact of an experience of the sublime, as "presumptive evidence of a future state of existence," was of more significance than the attempt to render this experience in poetry. Both as poet and critic, Wordsworth's primary concern was less aesthetic than moral and religious.[75] And

[73] *The Correspondence of Henry Crabb Robinson with the Wordsworth Circle*, ed. Edith J. Morley (Oxford: Oxford University Press, 1927), II, 820; Morley, *Henry Crabb Robinson*, I, 191; Morley, *Blake, Coleridge, Wordsworth, Lamb, Etc.*, p. 31.

[74] Havens, *The Mind of a Poet*, p. 220.

[75] As E. D. Hirsch remarks, "For both Wordsworth and Schelling ... the two realms [ethical and aesthetic] interpenetrate ..." (*Wordsworth and Schelling*, p. 108).

because he is more concerned with the experience itself, his "business is not so much with objects as with the law under which they are contemplated."[76]

Because he felt that the importance of an object or experience was its ability to set the imagination in motion, Wordsworth saw no need to make his poetry deal with what his critics believed to be objects or events worthy of great poetry. His aim was to select subjects within the range of man's daily experience, a practice that he defended in one of his essays "Upon Epitaphs":

> ... it is not only no fault but a primary requisite in an epitaph that it shall contain thoughts and feelings which are in their substance common-place, and even trite. It is grounded upon the universal intellectual property of man, —sensations which all men have felt and feel in some degree daily and hourly;—truths whose very interest and importance have caused them to be unattended to, as things which could take care of themselves.[77]

Except for *The Prelude* and *The Excursion*, wherein he attempts to *explain* these experiences, Wordsworth's poetry of imagination seldom deals with the grand and impressive objects and forces of Nature, but rather with apparently insignificant things like simple songs and greetings, solitary figures, and seemingly trivial boyhood experiences. Yet when he discusses the sublime in his prose, he associates these experiences with anything but ordinary persons and events —Milton's Messiah, Shakespeare's Lear, and the Bible— citing, in fact, much the same illustrations that Coleridge cites. The contradiction here is only apparent. Whenever he embodied these experiences in his characteristic

[76] *LY*, I, 184.
[77] *Prose*, II, 58.

symbols, Wordsworth felt no need to explain them; to him they spoke for themselves. When he did try to explain them, whether in prose or in verse, he fell back on a more conventional way of talking about the sublime that provided him at least with a vocabulary his readers would recognize. This is not to say that his prose discussions of the sublime in poetry are unrelated to his own poetic mode, merely that his experiences of the sublime had different origins and required different expression from those of the illustrations he cited. In their most important characteristics these illustrations and his poetry perfectly agree: both emphasize the moral and religious nature of the sublime and its ability to free the imagination from the senses by extending the latter to their limits. This is the point, says Kant, "when nothing any longer meets the eye of sense, and the un-mistakable and ineffaceable idea of morality is left in possession of the field. . . ."[78]

In his discussion of the conception of *Lyrical Ballads*, Coleridge speaks of "the two cardinal points of poetry, the power of exciting the sympathy of the reader by a faithful adherence to the truth of nature, and the power of giving the interest of novelty by the modifying colors of imagina-tion."[79] These two aims have sometimes been thought to conflict, and a belief that they do would naturally lead one to maintain, as Beatty does, that Wordsworth "regards this power of Imagination as having its origins, not in some far and mystic experience, but in the intimate and almost daily experiences which we all of us, even the least poetical, may know."[80] But this is a false dilemma, for to both Words-worth and Coleridge, and especially to Wordsworth, the

[78] Kant, *Critique of Aesthetic Judgement*, p. 127.
[79] *BL*, II, 5.
[80] Beatty, *William Wordsworth*, p. 163.

mystical, the experience of the sublime, may very well be produced by our "intimate and almost daily experience." In Wordsworth's poetry this is very often the case. To him the far and the mystic were by no means conjunctive; the mystical and the everyday, by no means mutually exclusive. The very opposite was his own theory and practice. In another passage from the *Biographia*, Coleridge writes that "The sudden charm, which accidents of light and shade, which moon-light or sun-set diffused over a known and familiar landscape, appeared to represent the practicability of combining both" the "two cardinal points of poetry" (II, 5). As Wordsworth's contributions to *Lyrical Ballads* were designed to demonstrate, there are sources of sublimity hidden from man by their very familiarity. There is no contradiction between what Coleridge calls "a faithful adherence to the truth of nature" and poetic renderings of mystical experiences, because Nature herself is charged with divinity and it is only man's familiarity with Nature that blinds him to it. In the experience of the sublime, something occurs to frustrate that familiarity. The obscure light of a moonlit night or of sunset softens the borders of things so that the senses are unable to distinguish separate items and limits (both functions that feed the false secondary power by which we multiply distinctions); separateness gives way to unity, and concepts of understanding to symbols of infinity. It is primarily the religious significance of such experiences that Wordsworth regarded as most valuable; thus he speaks proudly of "the spirituality with which I have endeavored to invest the material Universe, and the moral relation under which I have wished to exhibit its most ordinary appearances."[81]

[81] *Wordsworth and Reed*, ed. Leslie Nathan Broughton (Ithaca: Cornell University Press, 1933), p. 144.

The nature of that faculty of man which enables him to experience the sublime was never clearly defined by Wordsworth. In his poetry as well as his prose it is called both imagination and "Reason in her highest mood," and these two faculties are often identified. Rader's explanation of this fact is probably the best:

> It is typical of . . . [Wordsworth's] thought that he often does not clearly distinguish between reason and imagination; he refers to them as if they were two aspects of one faculty. The explanation is that he regarded both as the empirical manifestation of the divine and immortal part of man.[82]

This vagueness concerning the particular nature of the faculty of imagination or the "higher reason" is one of many problems that Kant bequeathed to his followers. Schelling, for example, admitted the limitations of Kant's "pure" reason (which, in English, came to be called the Understanding) and "practical reason" (the "higher reason" of Coleridge and Wordsworth), but claimed for the faculty he called imagination the power to intuit the reality beyond appearance, Kant's unknowable *noumena*. Coleridge too denied that man was powerless to know things in themselves, but retained the term Reason (as opposed to Understanding) to designate the faculty endowed with this power. Wordsworth, presumably because he was less concerned with precise terminology than were the philosophers, was content to claim that such a faculty exists, and to treat imagination and the higher reason as two terms for one ineffable power, whose presence he had experienced but could not really explain.

[82] Rader, *Presiding Ideas*, p. 157.

A mode of symbolism rooted in the empirical world of sense yet transcending it is the only method which Kant felt was valid for making noumenal reality at least partially accessible to man, and it is precisely this method that Wordsworth employed to express his intuitions of eternity. The world which we see is the real world, but its reality cannot be known until it is stripped of its familiar trappings and made to appear in a new—and necessarily dim—light. Then even the simplest things of Nature can become types and symbols of eternity; for, as Wordsworth is said to have remarked to Aubrey De Vere, "truth in its largest sense" is "a thing at once real and ideal . . . including exact and accurate detail, and yet everywhere subordinating mere detail to the spirit of the whole. . . ."[83]

Wordsworth's greatest poems are, in a sense, poems of failure; his symbols of infinity are not, because they cannot be, equal to the experiences that they are meant to communicate. "An IDEA," Coleridge writes, "in the *highest* sense of that word, cannot be conveyed but by a *symbol*; and, except in geometry, all symbols of necessity involve an apparent contradiction."[84] This is Kantian terminology and these "Ideas" are what Kant called "aesthetical Ideas," to which no "definite thought, i.e. . . . *concept*" is adequate.[85] Because this is true a great deal of criticism of Wordsworth's symbolism is irrelevant, or, at best, is misdirected at a particular poet when it should be applied to the nature of language itself.

Kenneth MacLean remarks that there are not one but two

[83] *Prose*, III, 488.
[84] *BL*, I, 100.
[85] Quoted in Theodore M. Greene, "A Reassessment of Kant's Aesthetic Theory," *The Heritage of Kant*, p. 347.

imaginations at work in Wordsworth's poetry. One of these is "the associative imagination . . . which lent itself to understanding"; the other is the higher imagination, which is not limited to concepts of the understanding but states its truths by indirection. According to MacLean, "When the ways of association take over," everything is "too plain" and "something has been lost."[86] In other words, the associative imagination produces poetry of rational statement, the higher imagination, poetry of untranslatable symbols. Essentially the same distinction was made by Kant, who was careful to distinguish between two kinds of imagination, the "productive" and the "reproductive." In the following passage from the *Critique of Pure Reason* he explains this distinction:

> In so far as imagination is spontaneity, I sometimes also entitle it the *productive* imagination, to distinguish it from the *reproductive* imagination, whose synthesis [of a sensuous manifold] is entirely subject to empirical laws, the laws, namely, of association. . . .[87]

Even closer to MacLean's account is the following passage from the *Critique of Judgement*, in which these two kinds of imagination are distinguished according to their cooperation with either reason or understanding, and in which the activity of the imagination under the control of reason is attributed to the sublime experience:

> The mind feels itself *set in motion* in the representation of the sublime in nature; whereas in the aesthetic judgement upon what is beautiful therein it is in *restful* contemplation . . . just as in the estimate of the beautiful imagination and

[86] MacLean, "Levels of Imagination," *PQ*, XXXVIII, 393.
[87] Immanuel Kant, *Critique of Pure Reason*, trans. Norman Kemp Smith (2nd impress.; New York: The Humanities Press, 1950), p. 165.

understanding by their concert generate subjective finality of the mental faculties, so imagination and *reason* do so here by their conflict. . . .

Elsewhere in this critique, in his discussion of the poetic imagination, Kant describes the very process that produced Wordsworth's symbols of infinity:

> . . . the imagination here displays a creative activity, and it puts the faculty of intellectual ideas (reason) into motion—a motion, at the instance of a representation, towards an extension of thought, that, while germane, no doubt, to the concept of the object, exceeds what can be laid hold of in that representation or clearly expressed.[88]

The most important similarity between Wordsworth's and Kant's theory of the sublime is their association of the sublime with the faculty of imagination working in cooperation with reason. In the *Critique of Judgement* Kant distinguishes carefully between "taste" and "feeling." The former he refers to judgments of the beautiful, the latter to judgments of the sublime. The first of the following passages is from this critique; the second is from Wordsworth's "Essay, Supplementary to the Preface":

> . . . we demand both taste and feeling [in making aesthetic judgements] of every man . . . in the case of the former, since judgement there refers the imagination merely to the understanding . . . we make the requirement as a matter of course, whereas in the case of the latter, since here the judgement refers the imagination to reason, as a faculty of ideas, we do so only under a subjective presupposition, (which, however, we believe we are warranted in making,) namely, that of the moral feeling in man.[89]

[88] Kant, *Critique of Aesthetic Judgement*, pp. 107, 177.
[89] *Ibid.*, p. 116.

Proportion and congruity, the requisite knowledge being supposed, are subjects upon which taste may be trusted . . . for in its intercourse with these the mind is *passive,* and is affected painfully or pleasurably as by an instinct. But the profound and the exquisite in feeling, the lofty and universal in thought and imagination; or, in ordinary language, the pathetic and the sublime;—are neither of them, accurately speaking, objects of a faculty which could ever . . . have been designated by the metaphor—*Taste.*[90]

The contradiction that Coleridge believed was inherent in all symbolism, except the artificial and ultimately unreal symbolism of mathematics, inevitably results when "the Infinite Being accommodates himself to a finite capacity" and when "poetry—ethereal and transcendent" is "yet incapable to sustain her existence without sensuous incarnation."[91] In language the truth of which any Christian platonist would recognize, when the Word is made flesh, it is no longer the Word in its pure state.

This inevitable incapacity of the imagination to find rational concepts to convey its intuitions should help us to understand at least two characteristics of Wordsworth's poems of imagination. The first of these, his choice of "mean," everyday objects and incidents I have already

[90] *PW,* II, 427.

[91] *PW,* II, 412. Wordsworth recognized that the effect of such incidents as his crossing of the Alps was two-fold and paradoxical. First came a terrible sense of man's littleness, then a feeling of his superiority based on his strength of imagination. To Coleridge's comment on the inherent flaw in symbolism cf. this remark from Ernst Cassirer, *Language and Myth*, trans. Susanne K. Langer (New York: Dover Publications, 1953): "For all mental processes fail to grasp reality itself, and in order to represent it, to hold it at all, they [men] are driven to the use of symbols. But all symbolism harbors the curse of mediacy; it is bound to obscure what it seeks to reveal" (p. 7).

discussed. The second concerns the peculiar nature of his symbolism. Because the poems of imagination seek to achieve from symbolism an effect of which symbols are incapable, Wordsworth frequently resorts to incantation, a favorite device of mystics in all ages and one more attempt to overcome the limitations of language by suggesting more meaning than words themselves can bear. Readers of Wordsworth will need no more than a mention of this device to recall examples of it. Perhaps the most striking illustration is in the opening lines of "The Solitary Reaper":

> Behold her, *single* in the field,
> Yon *solitary* Highland Lass!
> Reaping and singing *by herself*; . . .[92]

An even better known example is the opening of "Tintern Abbey," concerning which Tennyson complained of the repetition of the word *again* "four times in the first fourteen lines."[93] It is hardly necessary to remark that such repetitions

[92] Italics mine. The importance of solitude to Wordsworth's poems of imagination has already received careful study, notably in John Jones' *The Egotistical Sublime*. In part, this was Wordsworth's inheritance from earlier commentators on the sublime, who frequently by statement and illustration associated the sublime with solitude. In part, however, it was a result of Wordsworth's personal experience, for he was alone when most of his visionary experiences occurred. In his "Recollections of Wordsworth," Aubrey De Vere records this remark: "Scott misquoted in one of his novels my lines on *Yarrow*. He makes me write, 'The swans on sweet St. Mary's lake / Float double, swans and shadow;' but I wrote 'The *swan* on *still* St. Mary's lake.' Never could I have written 'swans' in the plural. The scene when I saw it, with its still and dim lake, under the dusky hills, was one of utter loneliness . . . . Had there been many swans and many shadows, they would have implied nothing as regards the character of the scene; and I should have said nothing about them" (*Prose*, III, 487–488).

[93] Cited in F. W. Bateson, *Wordsworth: A Re-Interpretation* (2nd ed.; London: Longmans, Green and Co., 1963), p. 187. For Wordsworth's defense of the technique of repetition see *PW*, II, 513.

are not merely due to Wordsworth's desire to record his experiences with minute accuracy. His purpose in using this device was to present his reader not only with the physical materials of the scenes described but with as much of his mood and spirit at the time of these experiences as his poetry could convey. Although her comment is not directed to this characteristic of Wordsworth's poetry, Josephine Miles gives an excellent description of its aim: "Thus art symbolizes, *by preserving the timeless moment*, and symbol like metaphor is, for Wordsworth, implied in the whole structure of the relation of time to eternity, not a literary device to be used in the indirection of idea."[94]

Given the fact that discursive language is inadequate to the task of communicating experiences of the infinite and given the inherent contradiction in all symbolism, Wordsworth chose not to disguise his revelations in conventional metaphor and allegory, but to try to preserve intact the spirit of the original experience. This is why he did not *explain* the significance of "the meanest flower that blows" and this is why his best poetry is essentially personal. Yet if Wordsworth was the most egotistical poet that ever was (to make explicit Hazlitt's implied contrast between Wordsworth and Shakespeare), his egotism is of a very special sort. It is the egotism of all mystics, who must, as nearly as possible, relate their experiences as they occur, in order to preserve something of their original purity.

There are really three kinds of poems within the class that Wordsworth called "Poems of the Imagination": those that *embody* experiences of sublime revelation, those that

[94] Josephine Miles, "Wordsworth: The Mind's Excursive Power," *The Major English Romantic Poets*, pp. 47–48. Italics mine.

comment on such experiences, and those that employ figurative language more conventionally (and often in a particularly eighteenth-century manner) for the purpose of more or less explicit statements of more or less definite "lessons." Most of this chapter has been concerned with the mode of symbolism that characterizes the poems of this first group, the symbolism of such poems as "There Was a Boy," "To the Cuckoo," "Nutting," and "A Night-Piece"; and such passages from *The Prelude* as the thefts of the bird and the skiff, the skating incident, the crossing of the Alps, and the ascent of Mount Snowden.[95] Examples of the second type of poem, that which comments on intuitions of the infinite, abound in *The Prelude*, wherein they serve to render discursively the mystical "spots of time" passages, and are also to be found in such poems as the "Intimations Ode," "Tintern Abbey," and "Star-Gazers."

Throughout this chapter, I have made it a point to distinguish carefully between poems that I have characterized as poems of imagination and those so designated by Wordsworth. I have done this simply because many of the poems included by Wordsworth in this group do not conform to his own comments on the nature and aims of the poetic imagination. Specifically, I would exclude from the

[95] *Prelude*, I, 317–325, 357–400, 425–463; VI, 560–591, 617–640; and XIV, 11–77. The relationship between the narrative of the crossing of the Alps and the apostrophe to imagination that follows is further illuminated by a comparison with other such accounts of sublime experience in the poem. There is a clear pattern in Wordsworth's use of these incidents in *The Prelude*: following each of the narratives are lines, usually introduced by an apostrophe either to Nature or the imagination, which comment on the experience related and seek to convey discursively the meaning that the experience itself has embodied.

category of imagination all those poems that appeal directly to the understanding and present explicit "morals," such poems as "Laodamia," "The Triad," and "Devotional Incitements"—indeed, almost the last third of the "Poems of Imagination" in the De Selincourt edition. More properly they belong with the poems of fancy. Between 1809, the date of his first known account of the classification and arrangement of the poems, and 1815, when he substituted for the earlier plan one very different in emphasis, Wordsworth suffered a decline in both his poetic and critical powers. For this decline (which, with varying dates, almost all scholars accept), many explanations have been offered, none wholly satisfactory. My concern, in any event, is not with the cause but with some particular effects of this decline.

One such effect (if it is not instead a cause) was Wordsworth's growing desire to *teach* in his poetry. The result is more comment and less mysticism. It is probable that the very waning of his imaginative faculty led Wordsworth (whose defensiveness was frequently commented upon by his contemporaries) to claim more and more of his poems for the imagination. When, in an American edition of the poems in 1837, Henry Reed expanded the class, "Poems of Imagination," Wordsworth was happy to adopt this alteration. Speaking of the first one-volume edition which he was seeing through the press, Wordsworth wrote to Reed in September, 1845:

> ... following your example I have greatly extended the class entitled Poems of the Imagination, thinking as you must have done that if Imagination were predominant in the class, it was not indispensable that it should pervade every poem which it contained. Limiting the class as I had

done before seemed to imply, and to the uncandid or unobserving did so, that the faculty which is the primum mobile in Poetry had little to do, in the estimation of the author, with Pieces not arranged under that head. I therefore feel much obliged to you for suggesting by your practise the plan which I have adopted.[96]

Whatever Reed thought of his alteration, it is likely that Wordsworth's enthusiastic acceptance of it was not as disinterested as he believed, but that he sought to refute the charge of Coleridge and others that his poetry had suffered a decline by enveloping in the ennobling cloak of imagination (still a term for which his contemporaries had great respect) the poems of his later years. Whether or not this is true, the great bulk of the poems added after 1815 to the class of Imagination were composed after the time which most critics fix as the *terminus ad quem* of his full poetic powers. Furthermore, the argument in this letter—that if imagination is predominant in the production of the poems as a group, it need not be so in the individual poems within the group—is a depreciation of his earlier elaborate efforts to distinguish between fancy and imagination. This possibility receives some support from the fact that Wordsworth more than once displayed a marked uncertainty over his own classifications of particular poems. On one occasion, for example, Crabb Robinson complained to him that "Laodamia," Robinson's particular favorite, was demeaned by its position among the "Poems Founded on the Affections" and asked that Wordsworth rectify his error by transferring the poem to the class of Imagination. In all editions after 1820 this poem appeared among the "Poems of the Imagination." Wordsworth's yielding to Robinson's

[96] Broughton, *Wordsworth and Reed*, p. 152.

request is revealing, especially when it is recalled that to Robinson *imagination* was usually a mere honorific term, meaning roughly the best, and that his argument for changing the category of "Laodamia" is based on the assumption that, in its original position, the poem belonged "to the inferior class of Poems Founded on the Affections."[97] To put this argument into correct perspective, we need only remember that included in this "inferior class" were "Ruth," a favorite of Coleridge, and "Michael."

Even before the decline of his poetic powers, Wordsworth had written poems of a kind far less demanding than the poems of imagination. When the higher reaches of art become increasingly inaccessible, he had the comfort of believing in the humble but real merits of his poems of fancy.

[97] Morley, *Henry Crabb Robinson*, I, 167.

7

Fancy and the Beautiful

For Wordsworth's admirers in every age, the poems of fancy have created special problems. What they meant to Wordsworth they have not meant to his readers, and they are today among the most neglected of poems.[1] Even their titles have the strangeness, though not the glamor, of the unfamiliar—"A Morning Exercise," "A Flower Garden," "On Seeing a Needlecase in the Form of a Harp." There are several reasons for the neglect of these poems, but two are particularly obvious: they are simply not as good as those better known, and they suffer from their classification as products of a poetic faculty inferior to the imagination. Still, Wordsworth cherished these poems and defended vigorously, though not always confidently, the faculty that produced them. Unlike Coleridge, whose comments

[1] For example, the excellent new Riverside edition of Wordsworth includes twenty-three poems from the class of Imagination and only two from the class of Fancy, one of which, "A Whirl-Blast from behind the hill," the editor feels should not have been so classified. He also notes correctly that "critics have never made much sense" of Wordsworth's classifications. *William Wordsworth: Selected Poems and Prefaces*, ed. Jack Stillinger (Boston: Houghton Mifflin Company, 1965), pp. 506–507, xviii.

on the fancy are uniformly derogatory, Wordsworth asserted that this power, when operating in its proper sphere, was capable of performing noble functions; he can even speak of it as aiming "at a rivalship with Imagination," without suggesting that such an aim is unreasonable.[2] A major purpose of his description of fancy in the Preface of 1815 was to refute Coleridge's implication that it is a faculty unworthy of true poetic genius.

Modern attitudes toward the fancy, particularly Wordsworth's fancy, have their origin in Coleridge, who lauded his friend unstintingly for possessing "the gift of IMAGINATION in the highest and strictest sense of the word," but had no words of praise for Wordsworth's fancy: "In the play of *Fancy*, Wordsworth, to my feelings, is not always graceful, and sometimes *recondite*. The *likeness* is occasionally too strange, or demands too peculiar a point of view, or is such as appears the creature of predetermined research, rather than spontaneous presentation."[3] Since the time of Coleridge's pronouncement, characterizations of Wordsworth's fancy have been consistently unsympathetic: fancy, "the energy of a mind engaged in aimless invention," is "untrue to fact," "frolicsome, and inferior" to imagination; it is a faculty that exercises a "facile, airy, and capricious manipulation of reality," and "where there is consciousness of fiction, it is the fancy" that predominates.[4] This picture of

---

[2] *PW*, II, 442.

[3] *BL*, II, 124. If Coleridge sounds here a bit like Dr. Johnson on the metaphysical poets, we should not be surprised. Many of his criticisms of Wordsworth are based on such Neo-classical principles as decorum and universality. On this point see chapt. 6, note 62.

[4] Willard L. Sperry, *Wordsworth's Anti-Climax* (Cambridge: Harvard University Press, 1935), p. 160; Arthur Beatty, *William Wordsworth: His Doctrine and Art in their Historical Relations* (3rd

the fancy is drawn from a random selection of modern critical opinion. It is a picture with almost no aberrant strokes.

Coleridge's conception of the fancy was in part the result of its gradual decline in the vocabulary of English aesthetics since Addison announced in his "Pleasures of the Imagination" that he would use the terms *fancy* and *imagination* "promiscuously." Addison is indeed scrupulously promiscuous and the modern reader finds amusing the predicability with which one term follows the other: if Addison writes "Fancy" in one sentence, "Imagination" is almost certain to appear in the next. Throughout the eighteenth century the terms continued to appear in tandem, but when a distinction was made or hinted at, it was almost sure to be in favor of imagination.[5]

Thus, Coleridge's condescending phrase "the play of Fancy" sums up the majority opinion of eighteenth-century critics, whose favorite adjectives for works later attributed to fancy are "sweet" and "gentle"—revealing terms

---

ed.; Madison: University of Wisconsin Press, 1960), p. 170; W. K. Wimsatt, Jr. and Cleanth Brooks, *Literary Criticism: A Short History* (New York: Alfred A. Knopf, 1957), p. 388; Basil Willey, *The Seventeenth Century Background* (New York: Columbia University Press, 1952), p. 301. See also Joseph Warren Beach, *The Concept of Nature in Nineteenth-Century English Poetry* (New York: The Macmillan Company, 1936), p. 182.

[5] See *Eighteenth-Century Critical Essays*, ed. Scott Elledge (Ithaca: Cornell University Press, 1961), esp. I, 206, 407; II, 713, 720, 886–887, 1019 1020, 1093, 1099; Wimsatt and Brooks, *Literary Criticism*, pp. 385–386; John Bullitt and Walter Jackson Bate, "Distinctions between Fancy and Imagination in Eighteenth-Century English Criticism," *MLN*, LX (1945), 8–15; Earl R. Wasserman, "Another Eighteenth-Century Distinction between Fancy and Imagination," *MLN*, LXIV (1949), 23–25.

certainly in a literary tradition so assertively masculine as the English.[6] With the elevation of non-rational processes that occurred in the second half of the eighteenth century, fancy became associated with that exclusively rational faculty called the understanding, while imagination was all but identified with the "higher reason," or, less formally, with the heart, the organ associated with direct (usually spiritual) insight into truth.

Earlier in the century imagination and fancy were usually discussed as if they were two names for one faculty, and they were almost always distinguished from more serious powers of mind, as rationalists in the Baconian tradition had insisted they should be. Even poets, with whose art these faculties were most often associated, were usually content to concede their separation from those mental powers devoted to the discovery of truth. Such a division of powers is implied in James Thomson's Preface to *Winter*, which argues that poetry should "at once *amuse* the fancy, *enlighten* the head, and *warm* the heart."[7] And almost a century later a reviewer of Wordsworth's *White Doe of Rylstone* refers disparagingly to "those subjects in which Pope and Dryden chiefly excelled, where the poet addresses himself to the fancy and understanding rather than to the heart"—a typical Romantic criticism of Neo-classical verse.[8] When it became common toward the end of the eighteenth

[6] To Coleridge's phrase "the play of fancy," used earlier by Archibald Alison (Elledge, *Eighteenth-Century Critical Essays*, II, 1019), cf. Kant's distinction between charming and serious employments of imagination, in *Philosophies of Beauty*, ed. E. F. Carritt (New York: Oxford University Press, 1931), p. 117.

[7] James Thomson, Preface to *Winter*, in Elledge, *Eighteenth-Century Critical Essays*, I, 407. Italics mine.

[8] *The Quarterly Review*, XIV (1815), 207.

century to distinguish between kinds of rational and kinds of imaginative faculties, reason and imagination were placed first in their respective categories (or simply confused or identified with each other), and understanding and fancy were consigned to minor roles in the formation of man's ideas and passions. While imagination was becoming the touchstone of great art, fancy continued to be associated with the *un*reality of imaginative activity, a fate reflected even today in our distinctly different connotations for the adjectives *imaginative* and *fanciful*. Wordsworth's high conception of the fancy was a marked departure from tradition; Coleridge's was more like that of his contemporaries. Modern scholars, including Basil Willey and R. D. Havens, have usually identified fancy with the understanding and imagination with reason.[9]

Coleridge not only associated fancy with an inferior mental faculty, but also with an inferior poetic mode, allegory, reserving for imagination the higher mode of symbolism. Shawcross draws upon *The Statesman's Manual* to explain Coleridge's distinction between these two modes: "For while the understanding 'in the blindness of its self-complacency' is content with allegories, which are nothing more than 'the translation of abstract notions into a picture-language'; religion ... has need of *symbols* for its expression. But the faculty of symbols is none other than the imagination...."[10] Thus linked to an inferior mode of poetic

[9] Basil Willey, *Nineteenth Century Studies* (New York: Columbia University Press, 1949), p. 28; R. D. Havens, *The Mind of a Poet* (Baltimore: Johns Hopkins Press, 1941), p. 465. See also Beach, *The Concept of Nature*, p. 149, and E. D. Hirsch, Jr., *Wordsworth and Schelling: A Typological Study of Romanticism* (New Haven: Yale University Press, 1960), p. 130.

[10] *BL*, I, lxxiii.

expression and a blindly complacent, narrowly rational faculty, fancy was bound to be excluded from Coleridge's conception of noble verse. As a servant of allegory, she was unfit to become a handmaid of Truth. As a modern scholar uncompromisingly puts it, fancy became for Coleridge a "wastebin" for all poetic activity in which imagination is not predominant.[11]

Even if writers of the late eighteenth century had not decided to elevate the sublime over the beautiful, circumstances peculiar to Coleridge and Wordsworth would have accounted adequately for Coleridge's coolness toward his friend's poems of fancy. Anyone who reads the *Biographia* and Coleridge's letters to the Wordsworths will agree that in a sense Wordsworth was meant to carry Coleridge's banner as well as his own. The letters of both men are filled with evidence of Coleridge's unselfish, almost fanatic devotion to Wordsworth's mission as the savior of English poetry. Time and again he interrupted his own work to further Wordsworth's, conducting negotiations with printers, reading proof and making corrections in copy, and everywhere advertising the New Poetry—all of those tasks that Wordsworth loathed. Coleridge's friends, notably Charles Lamb and Thomas Poole, thought his devotion a kind of idolatry, and it is true that Coleridge sometimes speaks of Wordsworth with the self-effacing zeal of a John the Baptist proclaiming the advent of a Messiah.[12] As his own poetic powers began to fail, Coleridge poured all his

[11] Barbara Hardy, "Distinction Without Difference: Coleridge's Fancy and Imagination," *EC*, I (1951), 336. See also a reply by L. J. Potts and Miss Hardy's rebuttal, *EC*, II (1952), 345–349.

[12] See *Collected Letters of Samuel Taylor Coleridge*, ed. Earl Leslie Griggs (Oxford: Oxford University Press, 1956–1959), esp. I, 215, 325, 327, 334, 391, 410, 582, 584.

ambitions into his faith in Wordsworth's greatness; quite naturally, then, he assumed a proprietary attitude toward the hero he had helped to create. Wordsworth accepted this devotion as his due—except in the reviews he met with almost no denial of his special powers—but he seems never to have appreciated the depth of Coleridge's disappointment when plans for the first truly philosophic poem of the age produced, instead, *The Excursion.*

In Coleridge's criticism, therefore, we deal not precisely with Wordsworth, but with Coleridge's image of him. A case in point is his attitude toward Wordsworth's fancy. Because this term had become associated with the gentler moods of nature and art, his admiration of Wordsworth as the most masculine of poets made him reluctant to credit Wordsworth's efforts in a mode somewhat feminine in its dependence on grace and charm. And since Wordsworth was for Coleridge the most philosophic of poets, anything suggesting playfulness had to be discouraged as the diversion of a natural genius for sublime undertakings. His plea that Wordsworth lay aside lighter tasks and "get on with The Recluse" echoes through his letters like a refrain, almost pathetic to the modern reader and probably irksome to Wordsworth.[13]

Generally, Wordsworth's friends who expressed opinions on his poems of fancy reveal more about themselves than about the poems. As might be expected, Lamb enthusiastically praised the poem which Wordsworth dedicated to him, "The Waggoner," called by Wordsworth a product of fancy. The kind but rather stolid Crabb Robinson, so delightful a foil for Blake's mock madness, was shocked that Wordsworth regarded so highly the poems of this

[13] *Ibid.,* I, 527, 538, 575, 1060.

inferior faculty.[14] Most important is Dorothy Wordsworth's opinion of them: she speaks of them with particular fondness. They seem, indeed, very much Dorothy's kind of poem, and she almost certainly had a great deal to do with their being written. Wordsworth's exclusively feminine inner circle of admirers encouraged him to look upon and to write about Nature's softer graces.[15]

Anyone who considers Wordsworth's defense of the fancy must contend with the poet's own ambivalent attitude toward this faculty. Though he gave the poems attributed to fancy a place of honor in his collected editions and catalogued its virtues in the Preface of 1815, he was capable of using the term as an apparent synonym for fiction ("The Danish Boy" is "entirely a fancy") and as an arbitrary power divorced from heart and head, hence from truth of any sort (he speaks of the need to separate expressions "merely of the writer's own fancy, from those which his judgment deliberately approves, and his heart faithfully cherishes").[16] This last comment was written in January, 1816, less than a year after his ambitious claims for the fancy appeared in his Preface of 1815. It is never thus with even

[14] *The Works of Charles and Mary Lamb*, ed. E. V. Lucas (New York: G. P. Putnam's Sons; London: Methuen & Co., 1905), VI, 519, 524–526; *Henry Crabb Robinson on Books and their Writers*, ed. Edith J. Morley (London: J. M. Dent and Sons Ltd., 1938), I, 96.

[15] There is no way to assess the influence on Wordsworth of such charming and gentle women as Dorothy, Mary, Sara Hutchinson, and Lady Beaumont in the years when most of the best poems of fancy were composed, but it was probably considerable. Dorothy and Mary —and his brother John for that matter—had a keen appreciation for the commonplace beauties of Nature, and Wordsworth expressed his love for these persons in such quietly charming poems as "To a Butterfly" ("I've watched you now"), "To M. H.," and "To the Daisy" ("Sweet Flower!").

[16] *PW*, II, 493; *Prose*, II, 9.

his informal remarks on imagination. When he uses the term imprecisely he identifies it mysteriously with the highest reason or with the soul of the universe. Even in the Preface itself, his adjectives for fancy are the customary ones—"playful," "amusing," "capricious," and the like.

Unless we are to dismiss his spirited defense of fancy in the Preface as one more example of his attempts at self-justification—akin to his excessive claims for "The Idiot Boy"—we must recognize at once a fact almost never recognized, that in Wordsworth's view there are two distinct kinds of fancy. Only one of these is well known: this is the willful and capricious faculty described in Book VIII of *The Prelude*. Arthur Beatty remains the principal source of information about this view of the fancy. Fancy, he wrote, is "the power of youth" that "Engrafted farfetched shapes on feelings bred / By pure imagination" (*Prelude*, VIII, 421–423). According to this interpretation, fancy was but an early stage of imagination.[17] Yet the poems classified by Wordsworth according to the predominance of this faculty were all composed in his maturity, and *The Prelude* itself, in a notable passage, implies the existence of a mature fancy quite different from that which is described in Book VIII:

> Yes, having track'd the main essential Power,
> Imagination, up her way sublime,
> In turn might Fancy also be pursued
> Through all her transmigrations, till she too
> Was purified, had learn'd to ply her craft
> By judgment steadied.   (XIII, 289–294, 1805 version)[18]

[17] Beatty, *William Wordsworth*, pp. 141, 201, 204.
[18] The important distinction between Wordsworth's mature and immature fancy is discussed by Bennett Weaver in "Wordsworth:

Wordsworth's description, in Books II and VIII, of his dawning creative powers implies that in youth there is no clear distinction between imagination and fancy. He speaks of fancy not as a separate faculty but as a wayward activity of imagination:

> ... when that first poetic faculty
> Of plain Imagination and severe,
> No longer a mute influence of the soul,
> Ventured, at some rash Muse's earnest call,
> To try her strength among harmonious words;
> . . . .
> . . . . there came
> Among the simple shapes of human life
> A wilfulness of fancy and conceit.   (VIII, 365–373)

In later passages of the same book he capitalizes "Fancy," but it seems less a distinct faculty than a personified tendency of imagination itself.

The creative faculties become distinct only in maturity, when the mind exercises its analytical bent and not so much recognizes a distinction as creates one. Thus matured, fancy and imagination were for Wordsworth not antagonistic but complementary powers, each providing an appropriate response to Nature, which itself manifests two complementary moods, in awful mountains and in daffodils, in tempests and in rainbows. Wordsworth's statements about Nature are everywhere permeated with its two "faces," and he thinks as naturally of pairs as Coleridge thought of triads: "the sweet breath of heaven" and "within / A correspondent breeze"; "My own voice" and "the mind's /

Forms and Images," *SP*, XXXV (1938), 433–445. In *The Prelude* (VIII, 249ff.) Wordsworth speaks of "Philosophy, methinks, at Fancy's call" as urging him on to his first love of Man.

Internal echo of the imperfect sound"; beauty and fear; fancy and imagination; Nature's "sister horns ... peace and excitation"; energy to seek the truth and "that happy stillness of the mind / Which fits ... [man] to receive it when unsought." [19] Most of these pairs, and others besides, dovetail into one, for they belong to one of two broad categories: the beautiful is somehow closely involved with serenity, peace, the understanding, and the fancy; and the sublime, with fear, awe, excitation, reason, and the imagination.

The progress of the fancy in Wordsworth's development was from the picturesque or grotesque to the beautiful. As it matured, it became a worthy partner of imagination, serving the beautiful and pathetic as the higher faculty served the sublime. Its special importance for Wordsworth has never been sufficiently emphasized, perhaps because the formidable example of Coleridge has prepared later readers of Wordsworth to apologize for or to ignore the poems of fancy.

Behind their disagreement over the value of fancy are profound differences in the experiences, poetics, and characters of Coleridge and Wordsworth. Coleridge's fancy had been developed and nourished almost exclusively from books, a circumstance that caused him to keep separate in his mind "real" objects and the products of a mind in reverie. Although he sometimes sounds like Wordsworth in the "conversation poems," his imagination even in these is restrained by the watchful eye of his analytic mind, and it operates with a degree of self-consciousness not at all characteristic of Wordsworth. Painfully aware of his

[19] *Prelude*, I, 33–35, 55–56; XIII, 1–10.

capacity for mental lassitude, Coleridge almost always identifies tranquillity with reverie, and reverie with indolence. Immobility is for him an image of horror—in the benumbed mariner, the bewitched Christabel, the agonized poet of the "Dejection Ode."

The concluding lines of "The Aeolian Harp" not only constitute a flaw in that poem but point to Coleridge's tragic distrust of imaginative vision. He begins by celebrating the joys of peace and serenity, and ends by denouncing the mental state that produced them because it creates "idle flitting phantasies" in his "indolent and passive brain." Nor is this poem an exception. Except for "Frost at Midnight" there is in all these "Wordsworthian" poems a most un-Wordsworthian expression of guilt for the poet's having indulged himself when there are promises to be kept that demand actions apparently antithetical to the pleasures of Nature and of poetic creation. Not until "Peele Castle" does Wordsworth sound this note of guilt, and he never seems, as Coleridge does even in "Frost at Midnight," to be willing himself into a faith in the tutorship of Nature and the spirituality of poetic sensibilities. If the almost desperate tone of these poems is recognized, Coleridge's escape into metaphysics seems inevitable. His cry of despair in the "Dejection Ode" over a dead Newtonian universe expresses not a loss of faith, but a confession that it never really existed for him.

Wordsworth paid high tribute to the fancy because he cherished tranquillity. For him the softer beauties of Nature evoked not guilt but peace, and in the poems of fancy he luxuriates in the charm and insouciance of Nature and the mind in their quiet moods. So important were these moods to him that he made of the group of poems embodying them something of a test for readers truly sympathetic to his poetry and character. He wrote to Lady Beaumont, "I am sure that whoever is much pleased with ... these quiet and tender delineations must be fitted to walk through the recesses of my poetry with delight, and will there recognize at every turn, something or other in which, and over which, it has that property and right which knowledge and love confer." The poems that he mentions feature the calm of Nature and the corresponding tranquillity of a mind in repose.[20]

Coleridge insisted that poetic creation and the experience inspiring it demand an energetic act of the mind, because he had no constant faith in Nature's power to speak even to the passive mind. Wordsworth valued equally the "sister horns" of Nature, "peace and excitation," and the analogous states in the mind of man, "That energy by which he seeks the truth" and "that happy stillness of the mind / Which fits him to receive it when unsought." Though they are to be found only in the "recesses" of his poetry, Wordsworth cherished his poems of fancy. He loved them, in fact, because they *are* less striking than the poems of imagination, just as he loved the mountains of the Lake Country for providing "a sense of stability and permanence that is, to many minds, more grateful" than the nobler feelings of sublimity excited by the Alps.[21]

Wordsworth habitually equated calm and permanence: he prefers to the "tumultuous harmony" of the nightingale the quiet song of the stock-dove, "Slow to begin, and never ending"; he praises the rustic cottages of the Lake Country for conforming to "that tranquil course of Nature and

[20] *EL*, pp. 129–130.
[21] *Prose*, II, 291.

simplicity, along which the humble-minded inhabitants have, through so many generations, been led."[22] Kant wrote that "beauty must find and maintain the mind in calm contemplation ... [and] can be united with charm and play of imagination."[23] Wordsworth's view is the same, and whereas Coleridge complained of Wordsworth's "play of Fancy," Wordsworth wrote these poems in praise of one of Nature's two equally valuable influences on the mind of man.

Probably, however, Wordsworth's delight in the lighter charms of fancy also hides a fear of his powerful, terribly exacting imagination."[24] Like the nightingale's song, the imagination is fiery and tumultuous. It fell upon him unawares and its visits were fleeting and unpredictable.[25] Wordsworth's matter-of-factness did not prevent his experiencing moments of imaginative vision, but it most certainly would have caused him to hold back a bit from so erratic a power as imagination. He must especially have felt mingled admiration and distrust for its ability to transform the solid earth into "An unsubstantial faery place." His love of simple things was both natural and self-protective, and his fearful worship of the sublime in Nature and the mind has its darker side in the eerie atmosphere of the Lucy poems and in the near terror of these lines on the theme of *The Recluse*:

> ... Not Chaos, not
> The darkest pit of lowest Erebus,
> Nor aught of blinder vacancy, scooped out

[22] "O Nightingale! thou surely art," ll. 4, 18; *Prose*, II, 265.

[23] In Carritt, *Philosophies of Beauty*, p. 117.

[24] For a cogent presentation of this thesis see Geoffrey H. Hartman, *Wordsworth's Poetry, 1787–1814* (New Haven and London: Yale University Press, 1964), pp. 17–18, 39–41, 333–338, *et passim*.

[25] It is interesting that in discussing the brief duration of mystical experiences, William James, echoing Wordsworth, speaks of them as

By help of dreams—can breed such fear and awe
As fall upon us often when we look
Into our Minds, into the Mind of Man—[26]

Even Blake must have shuddered. This distrust of rapture could also produce comic effects. For example, after a gloriously enthusiastic description to Dorothy of his first reactions to the Alps, comes this sudden, utterly characteristic return to the commonplace: "But I am too particular for the limits of my paper."[27]

Six of the poems of fancy were composed in 1802, a period of crisis for both Wordsworth and Coleridge. The best known poems of this year are the "Dejection Ode," "Resolution and Independence," and the first four stanzas of the "Intimations Ode." All three poems concern dejection and attempts to deal with it, and in all three dejection springs from regret over a lost power peculiar to childhood and youth. Coleridge's consolation is located not in his own restored imagination but in Sara Hutchinson's innocent joy and purity of heart. Wordsworth's consolation in the Ode is in the tie that binds the mind of man through all its stages and alterations, but in "Resolution and Independence" it comes from a reassessment of a mature poet's attitude toward youth and youth's imaginative powers. The danger of youth's visionary gleam lies in its unreliability, its fitful descent from extreme joy to extreme melancholy:

... it sometimes chanceth, from the might
Of joy in minds that can no further go,

---

fading "into the light of common day." *The Varieties of Religious Experience* (11th impress.; London: Longmans, Green and Co., 1905), pp. 380–381.
[26] "Prospectus" to *The Recluse*, ll. 35–40.
[27] *EL*, p. 33.

> As high as we have mounted in delight
> In our dejection do we sink as low.

Wordsworth's was such a mind, and in the introductory poem of fancy, also composed in 1802, he turns to the quiet, more permanent joys to be discovered by fancy in humble objects of Nature:

> In youth from rock to rock I went,
> From hill to hill in discontent
> Of pleasure high and turbulent,
>   Most pleased when most uneasy;
> But now my own delights I make,—
> My thirst at every rill can slake.[28]

The reason for Wordsworth's writing poems of fancy is of signal importance. The quieter charm of fancy was his insurance against the threat of tyranny posed by a hyperactive imagination:

> If stately passions in me burn,
> And one chance look to Thee should turn,
> I drink out of an humbler urn
> A lowlier pleasure . . . .

[28] "To the Daisy," ll. 1–6. Wordsworth telescopes in these six lines the account of his restoration described at great length in *The Prelude*. The first four lines describe him during the period just after he returned from France in 1792, when he approached Nature not in humble awe but "with microscopic view"; and lines 5–6 describe the attitude toward Nature of the maid (Dorothy or Mary) who "welcomed what was given, and craved no more" and helped Wordsworth to achieve a similar peace (*Prelude*, XII, 88–92, 151–158). A contemporaneous expression of Wordsworth's period "of pleasure high and turbulent" may be found in a letter describing his crossing of the Alps in 1790: ". . . again and again, in quitting a fortunate station, have I returned to it with the most eager avidity, in the hope of bearing away a more lively picture" (*EL*, p. 35).

In the daisy, and in the fancy, Wordsworth found that which he needed most when his imagination was most powerful: "A wisdom fitted to the needs / Of hearts at leisure."[29]

Book XIII of *The Prelude* opens with Wordsworth's hymn of thanksgiving to Nature for delivering him from the moral disease that impaired his imagination and taste. It is in these opening lines that he speaks of Nature's active and passive moods and of the analogous responses in man. He mentions both these moods, but goes on, in the remainder of this passage, to describe only one of them; he has been taught, he says, "to reverence a Power / That is the visible quality and shape of right reason." And this Power, which he may or may not have identified with Nature, has two principal functions: it "holds up before the mind . . . / . . . a temperate show / Of objects that endure . . ." and teaches him

> To look with feelings of fraternal love
> Upon the unassuming things that hold
> A silent station in this beauteous world.
>
> (XIII, 20–22, 29–32, 45–47)

There is no better description of the tone, themes, and subject matter of the "Poems of the Fancy." The daisy is an "unassuming Common-place" of Nature, a "sweet silent creature"; the celandine is a "Kindly, unassuming Spirit." And so throughout these poems there recur persistently tributes to the silent and meek creatures of Nature to whom the poet responds with "feelings of fraternal love" and the hope that he can make their virtues his own. Several of the poems of fancy were early grouped together in the edition

[29] "To the Daisy," ll. 49–52, 55–56.

of 1807 under the heading "Moods of My Own Mind," and
Wordsworth's defense of this group of poems is in effect a
defense of the fancy itself: "There is scarcely a Poem here
of above thirty Lines, and very trifling these poems will
appear to many; but, omitting to speak of them individually,
do they not, taken collectively, fix the attention upon a
subject eminently poetical, viz., the interest which objects
in nature derive from the predominance of certain affections
more or less permanent, more or less capable of salutary
renewal in the mind of the being contemplating these
objects?"[30] Here is at once a moral defense of these poems
and an implicit admission of their artistic shortcomings. His
greater poems, products of the imagination, are intrinsically
and individually artistic successes. The poems of fancy
depend far more on extra-literary responses and on an
arrangement of poems that permits mutual shading and
support to minimize weaknesses of execution.

Even readers who reject Wordsworth's distinction
between imagination and fancy cannot fail to recognize a
radical difference between the two groups classified according to this distinction. Such a recognition is implicit, of
course, in the consistent popularity of the first group and an
equally consistent neglect of the second. Many of the
differences are obvious, and a comparison of the two groups
will permit at least two generalizations: the forms, subject
matter, settings, and tone of the poems of fancy are more
conventional and traditional than those of the early poems
of imagination; but the differences between the early poems
of the two groups are much less striking than the differences
between the early and later poems *within* each of the two.
This last circumstance raises doubts about Wordsworth's

[30] *MY*, I, 127.

use of the two classifications after they were introduced in
the edition of 1815.

Differences of form are the most obvious. Only one of the
class "Poems of the Fancy" is in blank verse, and this one,
"Address to my Infant Daughter, Dora" was in every
edition from 1815 on placed last in the class, because it
"exhibits . . . [a] communion and interchange of instruments
and functions" between fancy and imagination, and therefore serves "as a preparation" for the class "Poems of the
Imagination." Of the "Poems of the Imagination" in the
last collected edition, twelve are in blank verse, and among
these are such distinctively Wordsworthian successes as
"There Was a Boy," "A Night-Piece," "Nutting," "The
Simplon Pass," and "Tintern Abbey." Obviously blank
verse was no requirement for poems of imagination, but it
is worth noting that most of Wordsworth's visionary
experiences occurred in his childhood and youth and that
most of his recollections of these periods were written in
blank verse.

The subjects of the poems of fancy, especially of those
composed after 1802, are not the sort that most readers
associate with Wordsworth. They are instead such subjects
as have always belonged to poets, and so conventionally
"poetic" as to recall Wordsworth's disdainful remarks in
the Preface to Lyrical Ballads on the "family language" of
poets.[31] His treatment of these subjects is so little distinguished from that of his predecessors that Hazlitt could,
with but little exaggeration, describe certain of the poems of
fancy as being "quite in the manner of [George] Wither."[32]

[31] PW, II, 387, 390–392.
[32] The Complete Works of William Hazlitt, ed. P. P. Howe (London:
J. M. Dent and Sons Ltd., 1930–1934), XX, 68.

Except for "A Whirl-Blast," discussed earlier in this book as a poem almost in the mode of imagination,[33] the subjects of the poems of fancy could be those of almost any seventeenth- or eighteenth-century nature poet; flowers and birds predominate, and all the poems feature the simple and relatively unimpressive objects and creatures of Nature. There are many more casual personifications than one expects to find in Wordsworth, and many classical references and allusions contrive to create an artificial style that Wordsworth might have been expected to condemn.

The two groups differ markedly in tone and atmosphere. The usual setting of a poem of imagination is painted in blacks and grays, desolate and gloomy. The scenes of most poems of fancy are bright and cheerful, the weather sunny and calm; in poems of imagination there are frequently storms or hints of storms.

John Jones points to the dissociation of moral and setting as a characteristic of Wordsworth's poetry after about 1805.[34] Actually, like most criticism of the later poetry, Jones' observation can be applied to even the early poems of fancy. In poems of imagination the poet's imaginative recreation of experience constitutes the moral significance of a poem. In poems of fancy experience and meaning are two things, sometimes skillfully fused, more often not. The philosophic foundation of the poems of imagination is a belief in the union of aesthetic and moral responses. Such a belief has been in every age the principal argument in defenses of poetry. After Kant, however, there came about

[33] See pp. 66–70, 79–80.
[34] John Jones, *The Egotistical Sublime* (London: Chatto and Windus, 1954), p. 135.

a new emphasis on the moral function of poetry solely in its capacity as art, in contradistinction to the separation of art into different and sometimes conflicting functions. The disintegration of most eighteenth-century descriptive poetry into scene and moral can be ascribed to the progressive tendency toward isolating the elements of pleasure and instruction in poetry. More and more, the "or" of Horace's dictum, *aut prodesse aut delectare*, came to mean that each part of a poem does not instruct at the same time that it pleases, as Renaissance critics had maintained, even less that it instructs *necessarily* in the very act of achieving aesthetic success. Kant, who assigned moral and aesthetic judgments to the same faculty of mind, and Wordsworth, whose Preface to *Lyrical Ballads* asserts that "We have no sympathy but what is propagated by pleasure," refused to give theoretical sanction to a poetry in which aesthetic and moral effects are disunited.[35]

Yet Wordsworth's poems of fancy are quite recognizably divided into story or scene and moral. Particularly in the later poems of fancy Wordsworth does not trust the experience itself to instruct the reader: morals must be stated explicitly. Moral and aesthetic purpose are clearly separate, and the art of the poem finds almost its only *raison d' être* in the moral message. One misses the condition of hushed expectancy that introduces an experience of ineffable revelation in the poems of imagination. In the later poems Wordsworth approaches scenes and objects with the cold-blooded design of extracting from them a sermon for his moral Muse.

A poem of this kind stands as the introduction to the "Poems of the Fancy" in the final arrangement of the poems.

[35] *PW*, II, 395.

In "A Morning Exercise," the lark is called "The happiest bird that sprang out of the Ark!"—appropriate enough description in a poem abounding in the imagery of matinal devotions. In a long apostrophe to the bird, Wordsworth sums up its lesson to man. The lark is "constant," yet "free," "humble" (by now a favorite virtue of Wordsworth's), yet "so ready to rejoice"—a glorification of the golden mean as distant in tone and substance from the "Characters of the great Apocalypse" as one could imagine. Opposites, indeed, are said to be "reconciled" in the lark, but they are only mildly in opposition and they are reconciled all too easily. The moral of the second poem of this class is left even less to the reader's imagination. "A Flower Garden," which encloses to protect, is an "Apt emblem (for reproof of pride)."[36]

Basil Willey finds the basic difference between Wordsworth's nature poetry and Thomson's *Seasons*, to which he says Wordsworth's poems bear a "superficial resemblance," in the fact that for Thomson, "The poetry exists to decorate, to render agreeable, a set of abstract notions . . . abstractions [which] have been taken over, as truth, from the natural philosophers . . . ." In contrast, says Willey, "Wordsworth's beliefs . . . were largely the formulation of his own dealings with 'substantial things'; they were held intellectually only because they had first been 'proved upon the pulses.'" Willey's contrast holds true for Wordsworth's early poems of imagination, but in all the poems of fancy acceptance of

[36] The theme of this poem, that "pure" freedom is a state of anarchy in which the sway of chance prohibits free choice, was a basic tenet of Wordsworth's philosophy at least from the time when he was rediscovering Milton's sonnets, and is reflected in his defense of poetic as well as political traditions and conventions. See, e.g., "Ode to Duty," the "Sonnets on Liberty and Order," and "Scorn not the Sonnet."

"abstract notions," particularly the traditional beliefs of Christianity, replaces truths imaginatively derived from personal experience. Willey states further that "Any translation of [Wordsworth's] experience into myth, personification or fable, though not necessarily always culpable, is inevitably a lapse towards a lower level of truth, a fall, in fact, from imagination to fancy."[37] The truths delivered by fancy are of a lower order than those of the imagination because the truths of the fancy are accepted from without rather than created within the mind of the poet. Or, to state the matter more accurately, in the strictest sense the fancy is not a faculty for discovering truths at all, but only for illustrating truths already accepted, not by the imagination, but by the understanding.[38]

The effects of this basic difference on the poems of imagination and of fancy are not difficult to discover. It is because fancy adorns values rather than creates them that Wordsworth characterizes it as a faculty that "does not require that the materials which she makes use of should be susceptible of change in their constitution, from her touch." Fancy makes no such demands because its materials already exist in the understanding in fixed intellectual values. Not so with the imagination: it does not work with materials of fixed meaning and value; instead, "She recoils from everything but the plastic, the pliant, and the indefinite."[39] For these reasons, there is a drama in the poems of imagination that is lacking in the poems of fancy. Fancy is on a leash, its limits circumscribed by the unyielding

[37] Willey, *The Seventeenth Century Background*, pp. 299, 305–306.

[38] Havens identifies as a characteristic of Wordsworth's later poetry his approaching Nature "with certain intellectual or ethical preconceptions" and finding "illustration or confirmation in the mighty world of eye and ear." *The Mind of a Poet*, p. 94.

[39] *PW*, II, 441.

truths which it can only illustrate by fable and emblem. Imagination is unlimited; its aim is to create value by transforming the materials on which it acts, to create of everyday objects and incidents symbols of eternity; not illustrating truths given to it, but yielding truths that defy illustration and the concepts that the meddling intellect would impose upon these truths. Instead of such symbols his poems of fancy offer overt moralizing, fables, and personifications. And either because in later years he failed to recognize the essential difference between these two modes or because he was no longer capable of the higher of them, he attempted to blur the distinction between the two powers that he had so carefully formulated.

This disregard of his classification could not have found favor with Wordsworth had he remained true to the characterizations of the faculty of imagination which are recorded in his essays and in *The Prelude*. Probably Wordsworth himself came to think of the terms *fancy* and *imagination* as mere labels denoting degrees of merit. Having accepted this simple view of the terms, it became his aim to justify his later productions by applying to them the now honorific title, "Poems of the Imagination." The change was gradual and of a piece with the decline of his poetic powers. Even in *The Prelude* of 1805, he could precede his great Simplon Pass episode, an example *par excellence* of the poetry of symbol, with this passage that owes its orientation to the "moral Muse" of eighteenth-century descriptive poetry:

> . . . With such a book
> Before our eyes, we could not chuse but read
> A frequent lesson of sound tenderness,

The universal reason of mankind,
The truth of Young and Old. . . . (VI, 473–477)

After this time the conventional glimpses into the Book of Nature grow more frequent and more dominant.

Despite his defense of fancy, Wordsworth was aware that its products are inferior to those of imagination. He was also aware that because the processes of fancy are "as capricious as the accidents of things," its activities are not firmly grounded in reality, and he knew that if fancy often "leads the pastimes of the glad," she can also "pervert the evidence of joy" by transforming innocent objects into grotesque nightmare images.[40] Within the poems themselves he is often at pains to distinguish between inherent qualities of natural objects and meanings imposed upon them by the fancy; whereas imagination is more trustworthy than the senses, fancy is less.

The charm and restfulness of the processes of fancy answered to a great need in Wordsworth's nature, but he never really trusted its methods. In the early version of *The Prelude* he credits fancy with the power to find in Nature "a genuine counterpart / And softening mirror of the moral world," but he retreats from that position in the revised text: now fancy is no longer said to discover meaning in Nature but to invent it, to produce "Apt illustrations of the moral world, / Caught at a glance, or traced with curious pains."[41]

In one of the poems of fancy Wordsworth looks back

[40] "A Morning Exercise," ll. 1, 12; *Prelude*, VIII, 365–423.

[41] For a discussion of Wordsworth's revision of these lines in its wider context see Earl R. Wasserman, "Nature Moralized: The Divine Analogy in the Eighteenth Century," *ELH*, XX (1953), 39–76.

nostalgically to a time when "Fancy was Truth's willing page."[42] He probably had in mind the early seventeenth century, the great age of emblematic religious poetry and the last period in Western civilization when almost all men shared a body of beliefs so strong that a poet could depend upon even a casual observation of Nature to yield moral truths and lessons. The way of imagination demands much more of a poet, but only imagination could work effectively as a moral instrument in an age that had seen Nature shorn of its divinity and divorced from the mind of man. The poems of fancy depended upon a settled, comfortable faith in the easy accessibility of the divine in Nature. In a sense they are Wordsworth's escapist poems, yet for all their artistic weaknesses they can have for modern readers the refreshing charm of an innocence that stubbornly resists powerful forces which must eventually destroy it. And among Wordsworth's poetry they decorate the charming recesses he described to Lady Beaumont; they are all the more appealing for their contrast to the pervading nervous excitement that challenges us in the greater poems.

[42] See pp. 75–76, and *Prose*, II, 59: ". . . alas! ages must pass away before men will have their eyes open to the beauty and majesty of Truth, and will be taught to venerate Poetry no further than as she is a handmaid as pure as her mistress—the noblest handmaid in her train!"

8

The Two Faces of Nature

Wordsworth once remarked that "Poetry is the image of man and nature." [1] This is a tantalizing statement that seems at once profoundly wise and ultimately inexplicable. It may be merely a cryptic nod to mimetic theory, and yet perhaps it expresses Wordsworth's awareness of something that makes him different from all other poets, an awareness that his life, his responses to the natural world, and the process by which his best poetry was created followed an identical pattern. This pattern, traced again and again in his autobiographical poems, is the core of *The Prelude* and of the most famous description of the poetic process in the English language. [2] It is also the key to understanding the relationships—personal, philosophic, and aesthetic—between the poems of imagination and the poems of fancy.

"Sublimity," Wordsworth wrote, "is the result of Nature's first great dealings with the superficies of the Earth; but the general tendency of her subsequent operations is towards the production of beauty. . . ." [3] Such was also the progress of Wordsworth's response to the natural world. In

[1] Preface to *Lyrical Ballads*, *PW*, II, 395.
[2] *PW*, II, 400–401.
[3] *Prose*, II, 245.

his childhood and youth he had "too exclusively esteemed *that* love, / And sought *that* beauty, which, as Milton sings, / Hath terror in it," until his reunion with Dorothy helped him to control and channel his wayward passions into a tranquil and peace-giving love: Dorothy helped to "soften down" that "over-sterness" (*Prelude*, XIV, 244–247).[4] The change wrought by Dorothy's quiet delight in Nature is described by means of vivid contrasting images that appropriately associate stages of human life with Nature's complementary moods:

> . . . but for thee, dear Friend!
> My soul, too reckless of mild grace, had stood
> In her original self too confident,
> Retained too long a countenance severe;
> A rock with torrents roaring, with the clouds
> Familiar, and a favourite of the stars:
> But thou didst plant its crevices with flowers,
> Hang it with shrubs that twinkle in the breeze,
> And teach the little birds to build their nests
> And warble in its chambers. . . .   (XIV, 247–256)

The subject of these lines is Wordsworth's progress from egocentric isolation to community, and the images signalling his change are those of the poems of fancy. By a kind of shorthand he sums up the differences in setting and temper between these poems and the poems of imagination. The first group of images depicts a man in a solitude both physical and emotional, in a setting severe and turbulent,

---

[4] On Wordsworth's progress from emphasis on fear to emphasis on beauty see A. C. Bradley, "Wordsworth," in *Oxford Lectures on Poetry* (2nd ed. repr.; Bloomington: Indiana University Press, 1961), pp. 125–126; R. D. Havens, *The Mind of a Poet* (Baltimore: Johns Hopkins Press, 1941), p. 626; Francis Christensen, "Intellectual Love: The Second Theme of *The Prelude*," *PMLA*, LXXX (1965), 69–75.

dominated by the impressive effects of the sublime in
Nature—cliffs, roaring torrents, and the awesome mystery
of remote clouds and stars. In the poems of fancy the poet
is in fact or in memory accompanied by those he loves,
imbued with "some new sense / Of exquisite regard for
common things, / ... with these gifts / Of more refined
humanity ... (XIV, 261–264).

The whole of this passage is intended to justify the
tutorship of Nature, which leads man "from joy to joy,"
each joy different from the last and each appearing in due
season. Even without resorting to the myth of pre-existence,
Wordsworth could ground his faith on the efficacious
transmutation of turbulence into calm. Demanding less of
Nature, he could demand less of himself, of his "self-
haunting spirit" (XIV, 284). His quest for final solutions
of sublime mysteries

>   ... of sense and soul,
> Of life and death, time and eternity,
> Admitted more habitually a mild
> Interposition—a serene delight
> In closelier gathering cares, such as become
> A human creature... (XIV, 286–291).

Neglected as they are, and inferior as they are to the
poems of imagination, the poems of fancy are essential to an
understanding of Wordsworth—not only in the years of
his decline and not only as illustrations of his artistic
weaknesses, but for understanding him at his best as well.
A faith in the value of unassuming, silent creatures and in
such simple dalesmen as his own Michael is the great
achievement that he celebrates in *The Prelude*. The theme
and even the words of the section of Book XIV that

describes his restoration are those of his two other greatest poems on the grand and the mild processes of Nature and the human mind. In "Tintern Abbey" and in the "Intimations Ode" the emphasis is on an exchange of prideful isolation for a humble love of man's fellow creatures; in both poems he praises a mature tranquillity that attunes him to "The still, sad music of humanity," has "ample power / To chasten and subdue," and gives to clouds at sunset "a sober colouring from an eye / That hath kept watch o'er man's mortality." The innocent child's inability to conceive of his own death at first engenders a confidence born of pride and self-sufficiency, but in the fullness of time helps to develop a "human heart" that accepts the sadness and the joy of a mortal among mortals. He speaks of this humanized faith, in *The Prelude*, as the result of his restoration:

> And so the deep enthusiastic joy,
> The rapture of the hallelujah sent
> From all that breathes and is, was chastened, stemmed
> And balanced by pathetic truth, by trust
> In hopeful reason, leaning on the stay
> Of Providence.... (XIV, 293–298)

Fancy was Wordsworth's "moral Muse," and what she chiefly taught is the lesson of the passages I have been quoting: humility, compassion, love for mortal man; sympathy and love for Nature's unassuming creatures; trust in Providence rather than, or at least more than, in private vision.

Critics generally agree that Book VIII of *The Prelude* does not show how love of Nature leads to love of Man.

In fact, most believe that Wordsworth's youthful love of Nature had almost the opposite effect, and we know that his bitter disappointment in mankind at the time of the French Revolution and the English Reaction sent him hurrying back to a Nature unsullied by the human presence. His vision on the Wye near Tintern Abbey excludes all that is human except Dorothy, who is virtually his alter ego; he admits only the smoke that *might* denote the presence of a hermit (smoke seen from a distance, in any case), and the wearying din of life among many people is transformed by memory and imagination into harmonious music "Nor harsh nor grating."

Youthful love of Nature made him intolerant of human imperfection. His unwillingness or inability to accept man for what he is, is obvious in the language he uses to describe the Revolution. He saw France not as a real place and the revolutionists not as real, and therefore imperfect, people; they were for him characters in a romance, and France was "a country in romance." Real events he prized "but little otherwise than I prized / Tales of the poets," and he and Beaupuy conversed as Dion and Plato. Instead of suffering Frenchmen he saw characters from romantic fiction— Angelica, Erminia, knights and satyrs.[5] Given the nature of his comments on the Revolution, it is odd that his famous lines on "The French Revolution" have been cited as proof of his firm attachment to the world of real and substantial things.[6] In fact during his period of emotional involvement

[5] See esp. *Prelude*, IX, 67–95, 198–208, 408–409, 454–465; XI, 109–112. Whether or not the Vaudracour-Julia episode in Book IX was intended to provide a catharsis of Wordsworth's guilt over his affair with Annette Vallon, it is one more manifestation of his "romantic" attitude toward France during his sojourn there.

[6] Arthur Beatty, *William Wordsworth: His Doctrine and Art in their*

with the Revolution his anticipation of a new France was as much the fabric of romance as other Utopian fantasies. He created from the historical events a work of fiction, convoking "From every object pleasant circumstance / To suit my ends" (XI, 153–155).

The love of man described in Book VIII is love of man at a distance, and the beauty of the shepherd's life was in Wordsworth's mind as stark and uncompromising as his surroundings: their existence was "rich in beauty, beauty that was felt," but beauty with terror in it—"images of danger and distress, / Man suffering among awful Powers and Forms" (VIII, 163–165). And when Wordsworth pauses in this book to give thanks to Nature for leading him on to love of man, he praises chiefly those powers "that seize / The heart with firmer grasp . . .": "snows and streams / Ungovernable," "terrifying winds," and "awful solitudes" (VIII, 218–222). At a distance man was "A solitary object and sublime" (VIII, 272), and the love thus produced was for the creature of a proud, solitary, and severe imagination that projected itself in human forms. Wordsworth was able to perform this act of self deception, as he later did in France, because of the plastic power of imagination and the emotional distance that he kept between the real shepherds and his imaginative recreation. What he learned to love in this stage of his life was simply the thrilling power of his own imagination:

> . . . hence the human form
> To me became an index of delight,
> Of grace and honour, power and worthiness.
> . . . this creature—spiritual almost

Historical Relations (3rd ed.; Madison: University of Wisconsin Press, 1960), p. 145.

As those of books, but more exalted far;
Far more of an imaginative form
Than the gay Corin of the groves. . . .   (VIII, 279–285)

These men, Wordsworth next reminds us, were only mortals after all—"husband, father," capable of "vice and folly, wretchedness and fear." But the man that Wordsworth created to love was purged of human frailty by a highly selective, though unconsciously selective, imagination: "Of this [man's natural weaknesses] I little saw, cared less for it, / But something must have felt" (VIII, 289–293). The last line carries little conviction.

Described in these lines is "the heart that lives alone, / Housed in a dream, at distance from the Kind." In "Peele Castle" this stage of egotism is condemned, but in *The Prelude* Wordsworth's more typical attitude obtains.[7] This state of isolation and self-containment is seen to have been appropriate for the stage in which it appeared; it is one of those needful disharmonies that was to be harmonized in the "calm existence" of his mature years. The more intense are the sensations and passions of childhood and youth, the

[7] Wordsworth's apparently unqualified rejection in "Peele Castle" of "the youthful poet's dream" (reading of the 1820 text) is a rejection of that belief in the unity of the human identity expressed in such poems as "Tintern Abbey" and *The Prelude*. Clearly Wordsworth did not hold this view permanently, for the Solitary's fatal error was to cut himself off from his past, a radical action symbolized in his forsaking England for America. See *The Excursion*, III, 809, 831–834. Writing to Thomas Poole in 1799, Coleridge anticipated Wordsworth's self-analysis in "Peele Castle": "My many weaknesses are of some advantage to me; they unite me more with the great mass of my fellow-beings—but dear Wordsworth appears to me to have hurtfully segregated & isolated his Being. Doubtless, his delights are more deep and sublime; but he has likewise more hours, that prey on his flesh & blood." *Collected Letters of Samuel Taylor Coleridge*, ed. Earl Leslie Griggs (Oxford: Oxford University Press, 1956–1959), I, 491.

more profound will be the humanized soul of the mature poet.

Wordsworth's early love of his image of man made him impatient with normal human imperfection. Amid the sublime scenes of Nature he had been able to create in his imagination men worthy of his demanding tastes. When Frenchmen and Englishmen acted like real men with real human weaknesses, he retreated to Nature, "more like a man / Flying from something that he dreads than one / Who sought the thing he loved."[8] And just as the sublime face of Nature had inspired him to create an image of impossible perfection as a substitute for real men, so an appreciation for the humble and commonplace creatures of Nature made him more tolerant of the weaknesses flesh is heir to. The role of villain in "Poems of the Fancy" is assigned to proud and egocentric creatures, and the common lesson of these poems is the need to love as equals the most humble of Nature's creatures.

The growth of the poet's mind was from fear to love, "To love as prime and chief, for there fear ends" (XIV, 163); and although both the sublime and the beautiful, pain and joy are necessary elements of human life, Wordsworth's illustrations of his mature love are confined to the gentler moods of Nature and the mind:

> . . . Behold the fields
> In balmy spring-time full of rising flowers
> And joyous creatures; see that pair, the lamb
> And the lamb's mother, and their tender ways
> Shall touch thee to the heart. . . .   (XIV, 170–174)

His procedure in the last book, in describing his attainment

8 "Tintern Abbey," ll. 70–72.

of maturity, is precisely the reverse of that in the first, which recalls his very early experiences. In illustrating how his childhood was "Fostered alike by beauty and by fear" (I, 302), Wordsworth turns almost exclusively to episodes in which fear is predominant. In the last book he subordinates fear and the sublime to the role of means; the end is a harmonious conjunction of love and the beauty of Nature that together create "The calm existence that is mine when I / Am worthy of myself" (I, 349–350). *The Recluse*, which was to be in a sense the experiences of *The Prelude* recollected in an even more profound tranquillity, tells the same story:

> . . . [Nature's] deliberate Voice
> Hath said, "Be mild and cleave to gentle things,
> Thy glory and thy happiness be there.
>
> .   .   .   .
>
> All that inflamed thy infant heart, the love,
> The longing, the contempt, the undaunted quest,
> All shall survive—though changed their office . . ."[9]

For Wordsworth, this change involved a chastening of his pride and an acceptance of his need for other people. Above all it meant a balance between the sublime and the beautiful, between excitation and calm. In his childhood, nourishment came unsought (*Prelude*, II, 7); in youth he sought Nature "For her own sake" (II, 202–203); and in maturity he achieved a balance that permitted him to respond equally to "Nature's sister horns." He learned that man needs both "That energy by which he seeks the truth" and "that happy stillness of the mind / Which fits him to receive it when unsought" (XIII, 8–10). *The Prelude* is the record of his

---

9 "Home at Grasmere," ll. 734–743, *PW*, V, 337.

successful quest for this equilibrium, and the complementary relationship between the poems of imagination and the poems of fancy, all products of his maturity, was proof for him that he had achieved the balance he sought.[10]

Most poems of fancy are written in the present tense and describe a general condition. Most poems of imagination are in the past tense and describe a specific event in a highly particularized setting. Other obvious differences of style and setting harmonize with this one: the poems of imagination are dominated by the unique personality of the first person speaker, while in most poems of fancy the speaker's personality is of little importance to the effect of the poem. Finally, almost all the poems of imagination are quite obviously autobiographical, recalling memories mainly from Wordsworth's childhood. Most of the poems of fancy present reflections and experiences occurring more or less at the time of composition, and these reflections and experiences, moreover, are unexceptional and unexciting. The experiences of childhood exhaust the capacity for

[10] In *Revaluation* (London: Chatto and Windus, 1962) F. R. Leavis identifies poise as one of the "distinctive characteristics" of Wordsworth's poetry (pp. 174–185); and in "Intellectual Love," *PMLA*, LXXX, Christensen demonstrates that "the terror of the child leads to the calm of the man . . ." (p. 70). For a discussion of "Resolution and Independence" as an example of the restoration of mental poise, see Anthony E. M. Conran, "The Dialectic of Experience: A Study of Wordsworth's *Resolution and Independence*," *PMLA*, LXXV (1960), 66–74. Appropriately the two "spots of time" in Book XII, which are offered to explain how Wordsworth's imagination was restored, are not, like those in earlier books, divided into narrative and reflection. Instead Wordsworth was careful to work into the structure of his narrative that dual consciousness, youthful and mature, which transformed fear into tranquillity. Cf. *Prelude*, I, 306–339, 340–356; 357–400, 401–416; 425–463, 464–475.

wonder in almost anyone, and the principal difference in our response to Wordsworth's two major classes of poems is explained as simply as that. Because they lack this sense of wonder, the poems of fancy seem less "true" to us. In reading them we are not engaged in a process that communicates some special truth, because we feel that the poet himself is not so engaged. The reasons for our dissatisfaction with these poems are only partially accessible to analytic criticism. The stronger reason, of which we are usually not aware, is that we are still for all our modern skepticism spiritual descendents of Wordsworth and Coleridge. We do not respond warmly to the poems of fancy for the same reason that the Romantic poets came to censure eighteenth-century descriptive verse. We miss in the products of fancy a sense of authenticity, "a guarantee that the poem is an authentic experience which gives birth to an idea rather than the illustration of a ready-made idea."[11]

Since Wordsworth's later poems, even those that he included in the class of Imagination, have much more in common with the poems of fancy than with the poems of imagination published in 1815, we are justified in reversing Arthur Beatty's judgment that imagination was the dominant poetic faculty in Wordsworth's maturity. Above all, we should realize that the poems of fancy are quite as aptly called "Wordsworthian" as are the poems of imagination. In fact the greatest, most Wordsworthian poem of them all is a triumph of imagination that sings the praises of fancy. *The Prelude* affirms the value of the very change in Wordsworth's temper which was undermining his peculiar genius

[11] Robert Langbaum, *The Poetry of Experience* (New York: W. W. Norton and Company, 1963), p. 48.

even as he welcomed the calm existence of his later years. His greater tolerance for human limitations permitted him to make fewer demands on himself; and his more catholic acceptance of human and of natural creatures liberated him from the power of a poetic faculty and a mode of composition that probably would have soon exhausted his store of physical and emotional energy. At the height of his creative powers his letters and Dorothy's are often a catalogue of cruel pains and illnesses, but his later life was, despite several personal tragedies, an image of peace. The poems of imagination record the quest for tranquillity and the poems of fancy describe the happy result of this quest.

Appendix A

In the table below, showing Wordsworth's rearrangement in 1800 of poems that had previously appeared in the 1798 edition of *Lyrical Ballads*, I have altered some titles in conformity with those of the Oxford Standard Authors edition of Wordsworth's poems, edited by Thomas Hutchinson.

Order of Poems in *Lyrical Ballads* (1798)

   I   The Rime Of The Ancient Mariner
   II The Foster-Mother's Tale
   III Lines Left Upon A Seat In A Yew-tree . . .
   IV The Nightingale [in some copies *Lewti* appears in this position]
   V   The Female Vagrant [now a part of *Guilt And Sorrow*]
   VI Goody Blake And Harry Gill
   VII Lines Written At A Small Distance From My House [now entitled *To My Sister*]
   VIII Simon Lee
   IX Anecdote For Fathers
   X   We Are Seven
   XI Lines Written In Early Spring

XII   The Thorn
XIII   The Last Of The Flock
XIV   The Dungeon
XV   The Mad Mother [now entitled *Her Eyes Are Wild*]
XVI   The Idiot Boy
XVII   Lines Written Near Richmond ... [Beginning in 1800 published as two poems, now entitled *Lines Written While Sailing* ... and *Remembrance Of Collins* ...]
XVIII   Expostulation And Reply
XIX   The Tables Turned
XX   Old Man Travelling [later entitled *Animal Tranquillity And Decay*]
XXI   The Complaint Of A Forsaken Indian Woman
XXII   The Convict [omitted after first edition]
XXIII   Tintern Abbey

Order of the Poems of Volume One in *Lyrical Ballads* (1800)

I   Expostulation And Reply
II   The Tables Turned
III   Animal Tranquillity And Decay
IV   The Complaint Of A Forsaken Indian Woman
V   The Last Of The Flock
VI   Lines Left Upon A Seat In A Yew-tree ...
VII   The Foster-Mother's Tale
VIII   Goody Blake And Harry Gill
IX   The Thorn
X   We Are Seven
XI   Anecdote For Fathers
XII   To My Sister

Appendix B

The table below shows the arrangement of poems included in the classes of Fancy and Imagination in all editions of the collected poems supervised by Wordsworth, except for the last one, the edition of 1849–1850, which is the basis for the definitive modern edition of De Selincourt and Darbishire. Titles vary from one edition to the next, and occasionally even within an edition. For convenience and consistency, therefore, I have used throughout the titles that appear in the Oxford Standard Authors edition of Thomas Hutchinson. After their first appearance in this table, I have abbreviated the titles of a few poems in subsequent listings.

EDITION OF 1815

Poems of the Fancy

I	To The Daisy ["In youth from rock to rock I went"]
II	"A Whirl-Blast from behind the hill"
III	"With how sad steps, O Moon"
IV	The Green Linnet
V	To The Small Celandine
VI	To The Same Flower
VII	The Waterfall And The Eglantine
VIII	The Oak And The Broom

Poems of the Imagination

EDITION OF 1820

Poems of the Fancy

EDITIONS OF 1827 AND 1832*

Poems of the Fancy

* In the edition of 1832, "The Triad" is printed, without a number, between poems numbered XXV and XXVI of the "Poems of the Imagination."

Poems of the Imagination

EDITION OF 1836–1837

Poems of the Fancy

Poems of the Imagination

EDITION OF 1845 (IN ONE VOLUME)

Poems of the Fancy

Poems of the Imagination

Selected Bibliography

Texts and Primary Sources

WORDSWORTH

Early Letters of William and Dorothy Wordsworth. Edited by Ernest de Selincourt. Oxford: Oxford University Press, 1935.

The Letters of William and Dorothy Wordsworth: The Later Years. Edited by Ernest de Selincourt. 3 vols. Oxford: Oxford University Press, 1939.

The Letters of William and Dorothy Wordsworth: The Middle Years. Edited by Ernest de Selincourt. 2 vols. Oxford: Oxford University Press, 1937.

Poems. 2 vols. London: Longman, Hurst, Rees, Orme, and Brown, 1815.

The Poetical Works of William Wordsworth. Edited by Ernest de Selincourt and Helen Darbishire. rev. ed. 5 vols. Oxford: Oxford University Press, 1952–1959.

The Prelude. Edited by Ernest de Selincourt and revised by Helen Darbishire. 2nd ed. Oxford: Oxford University Press, 1959.

The Prose Works of William Wordsworth. Edited by Alexander B. Grosart. 3 vols. London: Edward Moxon, 1876.

Prose Works of William Wordsworth. Edited by William Knight. 2 vols. London: Macmillan and Co., 1896.

Wordsworth and Reed: The Poet's Correspondence with his American Editor, 1836–1850. Edited by Leslie Nathan Broughton. Ithaca: Cornell University Press, 1933.

AND OTHERS

Burke, Edmund. *A Philosophical Enquiry into the Origin of our Ideas of the Sublime and Beautiful.* Edited by J. T. Boulton. London: Routledge and Kegan Paul; New York: Columbia University Press, 1958.

Coleridge, Samuel Taylor. *Biographia Literaria.* Edited by J. Shawcross. rev. ed. 2 vols. London: Oxford University Press, 1962.

——. *Coleridge's Shakespearean Criticism.* Edited by Thomas Middleton Raysor. 2nd ed. 2 vols. London: J. M. Dent and Sons Ltd., 1961.

——. *Collected Letters of Samuel Taylor Coleridge.* Edited by Earl Leslie Griggs. 4 vols. Oxford: Oxford University Press, 1956–1959.

——. *The Complete Works of Samuel Taylor Coleridge.* Edited by W. G. T. Shedd. 7 vols. New York: Harper and Brothers, 1868–1871.

——. *The Literary Remains of Samuel Taylor Coleridge.* Edited by Henry Nelson Coleridge. 4 vols. London: William Pickering, 1839.

——. *The Table Talk and Omniana of Samuel Taylor Coleridge.* Arranged and edited by T. Ashe. London: George Bell and Sons, 1888.

De Quincey, Thomas. *Literary Reminiscences.* Boston: Houghton, Mifflin and Company, 1882.

Hazlitt, William. *The Complete Works of William Hazlitt.* Edited by P. P. Howe. 21 vols. London: J. M. Dent and Sons Ltd., 1930–1934.

Kant, Immanuel. *Critique of Aesthetic Judgement.* Translated and with introductory essays by James Creed Meredith. Oxford: Oxford University Press, 1911.

——. *Critique of Pure Reason.* Translated by Norman Kemp Smith. 2nd impress. repr. New York: The Humanities Press, 1950.

Robinson, Henry Crabb. *Blake, Coleridge, Wordsworth, Lamb, Etc.* Edited by Edith J. Morley. Manchester: Manchester University Press, 1922.

———. *The Correspondence of Henry Crabb Robinson with the Wordsworth Circle.* Edited by Edith J. Morley. 2 vols. Oxford: Oxford University Press, 1927.

———. *Henry Crabb Robinson on Books and their Writers.* Edited by Edith J. Morley. 2 vols. London: J. M. Dent and Sons Ltd., 1938.

Wordsworth, Dorothy. *Journals of Dorothy Wordsworth.* Edited by Ernest de Selincourt. 2 vols. New York: The Macmillan Company, 1941.

Critical and Other Works
WORDSWORTH

Abercrombie, Lascelles. *The Art of Wordsworth.* London: Oxford University Press, 1952.

Arnold, Matthew. Preface to *Poems of Wordsworth.* London: Macmillan and Co., 1879.

Banerjee, Srikumar. *Critical Theories and Poetic Practice in the "Lyrical Ballads."* London: Williams and Norgate Ltd., 1931.

Bateson, F. W. *Wordsworth: A Re-Interpretation.* 2nd. ed. London: Longmans, Green and Co., 1963.

Beatty, Arthur. *William Wordsworth: His Doctrine and Art in their Historical Relations.* 3rd. ed. Madison: University of Wisconsin Press, 1960.

Christensen, Francis. "Intellectual Love: The Second Theme of *The Prelude,*" *PMLA,* LXXX (March 1965), 69–75.

Clarke, C. C. *Romantic Paradox.* New York: Barnes and Noble Inc., 1963.

Conran, Anthony E. M. "The Dialectic of Experience: A Study of Wordsworth's *Resolution and Independence,*" *PMLA,* LXXV (March 1960), 66–74.

Dowden, Edward. Preface to *The Poetical Works of William Wordsworth*. 7 vols. London: George Bell and Sons, 1892–1893.

Ferry, David. *The Limits of Mortality*. Middletown: Wesleyan University Press, 1959.

Garrod, H. W. *Wordsworth: Lectures and Essays*. Oxford: Oxford University Press, 1923.

Harper, George McLean. *William Wordsworth: His Life, Works, and Influence*. 2 vols. New York: Charles Scribner's Sons, 1916.

Hartman, Geoffrey H. "Wordsworth's *Descriptive Sketches* and the Growth of a Poet's Mind," *PMLA*, LXXVI (December 1961), 519–527.

———. *Wordsworth's Poetry, 1787–1814*. New Haven and London: Yale University Press, 1964.

Havens, Raymond Dexter. *The Mind of a Poet*. Baltimore: Johns Hopkins Press, 1941.

Hirsch, E. D., Jr. *Wordsworth and Schelling: A Typological Study of Romanticism*. New Haven: Yale University Press, 1960.

Hutchinson, Thomas. Preface to *The Poetical Works of Wordsworth*. London: Oxford University Press, 1932.

Jones, John. *The Egotistical Sublime*. London: Chatto and Windus, 1954.

Knight, William. Preface to *The Poetical Works of William Wordsworth*. 8 vols. Edinburgh: William Paterson, 1882–1886.

Lindenberger, Herbert A. *On Wordsworth's "Prelude."* Princeton: Princeton University Press, 1963.

Logan, James V. *Wordsworthian Criticism: A Guide and Bibliography*. Columbus: Ohio State University Press, 1947.

Lyon, Judson S. *The Excursion: A Study*. New Haven: Yale University Press, 1950.

MacLean, Kenneth. "Levels of Imagination in Wordsworth's *Prelude* (1805)," *PQ*, XXXVIII (October 1959), 385–400.

Miles, Josephine. *Wordsworth and the Vocabulary of Emotion.* University of California Publications in English, XII. Berkeley and Los Angeles: University of California Press, 1942.

Parrish, Stephen Maxfield. "Dramatic Technique in the *Lyrical Ballads*," *PMLA*, LXXIV (March 1959), 85–97.

———. "'The Thorn': Wordsworth's Dramatic Monologue," *ELH*, XXIV (June 1957), 153–163.

———. "Wordsworth and Coleridge on Meter," *Journal of English and Germanic Philology*, LIX (January 1960), 41–49.

———. "The Wordsworth-Coleridge Controversy," *PMLA*, LXXIII (September 1958), 367–374.

Perkins, David. *Wordsworth and the Poetry of Sincerity.* Cambridge: Harvard University Press, 1964.

Rader, Melvin. *Presiding Ideas in Wordsworth's Poetry.* University of Washington Publications in Language and Literature, VIII, 2. Seattle: University of Washington Press, 1931.

Raleigh, Walter. *Wordsworth.* 2nd impress. London: Edward Arnold, 1903.

Read, Herbert. *Wordsworth.* London: Jonathan Cape, 1930.

Reed, Henry. Preface to *The Complete Poetical Works of William Wordsworth.* Philadelphia: James Kay, Jun. and Brother, 1837.

Review of Wordsworth's *Poems* of 1815. *The Monthly Review*, LXXVIII (November 1815), 225–238.

———. *The Quarterly Review*, XIV (October 1815), 201–225.

Salvesen, Christopher. *The Landscape of Memory: A Study of Wordsworth's Poetry.* Lincoln: University of Nebraska Press, 1965.

Smith, Elsie. *An Estimate of William Wordsworth by his Contemporaries.* Oxford: Basil Blackwell, 1932.

Sperry, Willard L. *Wordsworth's Anti-Climax.* Cambridge: Harvard University Press, 1935.

Thorpe, Clarence D. "The Imagination: Coleridge *versus* Wordsworth," *PQ*, XVIII (January 1939), 1–18.

Tribute to Wordsworth. Edited by Muriel Spark and Derek Stanford. London and New York: Wingate, 1950.

Weaver, Bennett. "Wordsworth: Forms and Images," *SP*, XXXV (July 1938), 433–445.

Wordsworth: Centenary Studies. Edited by Gilbert T. Dunklin. Princeton: Princeton University Press, 1951.

Wordsworth, Christopher. *Memoirs of William Wordsworth.* 2 vols. London: Edward Moxon, 1851.

Worthington [Smyser], Jane. *Wordsworth's Reading of Roman Prose.* New Haven: Yale University Press, 1946.

GENERAL

Abrams, Meyer H. *The Mirror and the Lamp.* New York: W. W. Norton and Company, 1958.

Beach, Joseph Warren. *The Concept of Nature in Nineteenth-Century English Poetry.* New York: The Macmillan Company, 1936.

Benziger, James. *Images of Eternity.* Carbondale: Southern Illinois University Press, 1962.

Bradley, A. C. *A Miscellany.* London: Macmillan and Co. Ltd., 1929.

———. *Oxford Lectures on Poetry.* 2nd ed. repr. Bloomington: Indiana University Press, 1961.

Bullitt, John and Walter Jackson Bate. "Distinctions between Fancy and Imagination in Eighteenth-Century English Criticism," *MLN*, LX (January 1945), 8–15.

Cassirer, Ernst. *Language and Myth.* Translated by Susanne K. Langer. New York: Dover Publications, 1953.

Criticism: The Major Texts. Edited by Walter Jackson Bate. New York: Harcourt, Brace and Company, 1952.

Eighteenth-Century Critical Essays. Edited by Scott Elledge. 2 vols. Ithaca: Cornell University Press, 1961.

Freeman, Rosemary. *English Emblem Books*. London: Chatto and Windus, 1948.

Gilbert, Katharine Everett and Helmut Kuhn. *A History of Esthetics*. New York: The Macmillan Company, 1939.

Hardy, Barbara. "Distinction Without Difference: Coleridge's Fancy and Imagination," *EC*, I (October 1951), 336–344.

———. "Imagination and Fancy," *EC*, II (July 1952), 347–349.

Henn, T. R. *Longinus and English Criticism*. Cambridge: Cambridge University Press, 1934.

The Heritage of Kant. Edited by George Tapley Whitney and David F. Bowers. Princeton: Princeton University Press, 1939.

Hipple, Walter John, Jr. *The Beautiful, the Sublime, & the Picturesque in Eighteenth-Century British Aesthetic Theory*. Carbondale: Southern Illinois University Press, 1957.

Hunt, Leigh. Preface to *Imagination and Fancy; or Selections from the English Poets*. American ed. New York: George P. Putnam, 1850.

James, William. *The Varieties of Religious Experience*. 11th impress. London: Longmans, Green and Co., 1905.

Kermode, Frank. *Romantic Image*. London: Routledge and Kegan Paul Ltd., 1957.

Knight, G. Wilson. *The Starlit Dome*. London: Oxford University Press, 1941.

Kroeber, Karl. *Romantic Narrative Art*. Madison: University of Wisconsin Press, 1960.

Langbaum, Robert. *The Poetry of Experience*. New York: W. W. Norton and Company, 1963.

Langer, Susanne K. *Philosophy in a New Key*. 2nd ed. Cambridge: Harvard University Press, 1951.

Leavis, F. R. *Revaluation*. London: Chatto and Windus, 1962.

Lyon, Judson S. "Romantic Psychology and the Inner Senses: Coleridge," *PMLA*, LXXXI (June 1966), 246–260.

The Major English Romantic Poets. Edited by Clarence D.

Thorpe, Carlos Baker, and Bennett Weaver. Carbondale: Southern Illinois University Press, 1957.

Miles, Josephine. *Eras and Modes in English Poetry.* Berkeley and Los Angeles: University of California Press, 1957.

Monk, Samuel H. *The Sublime: A Study of Critical Theories in XVIII-Century England.* New York: Modern Language Association of America, 1935.

Nemerov, Howard. *Poetry and Fiction: Essays.* New Brunswick: Rutgers University Press, 1963.

Peckham, Morse. "Toward a Theory of Romanticism," *PMLA,* LXVI (March 1951), 5–23.

————. "Toward a Theory of Romanticism: II. Reconsiderations," *Studies In Romanticism,* I (Autumn 1961), 1–8.

Perkins, David. *The Quest for Permanence.* Cambridge: Harvard University Press, 1959.

Philosophies of Beauty. Edited by E. F. Carritt. New York: Oxford University Press, 1931.

Piper, H. W. *The Active Universe.* London: University of London, Athlone Press, 1962.

Potts, L. J. "Imagination and Fancy," *EC,* II (July 1952), 345–347.

Roston, Murray. *Prophet and Poet: The Bible and the Growth of Romanticism.* Evanston: Northwestern University Press, 1965.

Stallknecht, Newton P. *Strange Seas of Thought.* Durham: Duke University Press, 1945.

Stevens, Wallace. *The Necessary Angel.* New York: Alfred A. Knopf, 1951.

Studies in Criticism and Aesthetics, 1660–1800. Edited by Howard A. Anderson and John S. Shea. Minneapolis: University of Minnesota Press, 1966.

Tuveson, Ernest Lee. *The Imagination as a Means of Grace.* Berkeley and Los Angeles: University of California Press, 1960.

Wasserman, Earl R. "Another Eighteenth-Century Distinction between Fancy and Imagination," *MLN*, LXIV (January 1949), 23–25.

———. "Nature Moralized: The Divine Analogy in the Eighteenth Century," *ELH*, XX (March 1953), 39–76.

———. *The Subtler Language*. Baltimore: Johns Hopkins Press, 1959.

Watson, John. *Schelling's Transcendental Idealism*. Chicago: S. C. Griggs and Company, 1882.

Wellek, René. *A History of Modern Criticism*. 3 vols. New Haven: Yale University Press, 1955.

Willey, Basil. *The Eighteenth Century Background*. London: Chatto and Windus, 1949.

———. *Nineteenth Century Studies*. New York: Columbia University Press, 1949.

———. *The Seventeenth Century Background*. New York: Columbia University Press, 1952.

Willoughby, L. A. "English Romantic Criticism," *Weltliteratur: Festgabe für Fritz Strich*. Edited by Walter Henzen, Walter Muschg, and Emil Staiger. Bern: Francke Verlag, 1952.

Wimsatt, W. K., Jr. and Cleanth Brooks. *Literary Criticism: A Short History*. New York: Alfred A. Knopf, 1957.

Wordsworth and Coleridge: Studies in honor of George McLean Harper. Edited by Earl Leslie Griggs. Princeton: Princeton University Press, 1939.

Index